L. Constance

Zurich

VORARL[...]

igi

Arlberg

[...]ck

[...] ALPS

Brenner P.

OETZTAL ALPS

vorder Rhein

Chur

Dissis

Stelvio P.

Meran

St Gotth. P.

Rheinwaldhorn

Splugen P.

ORTLER ALPS

Bolzano

Marmolata

Pontresina

Maloja P.

Meira

Bernino

Adda

Adamello

Cima Tosa

Avisio

Etsch

DOLOMITES

Lugano

L. Como

Trento

L. Maggiore

BERGAMESQUE ALPS

L. Iseo

L. Garda

Verona

Po

Adige

Genoa

The Alps
West & Central

Gulf of Genoa

0 5 10 20 30 40 50 60

scale of miles

THE ALPS

1 Mont Blanc

*From the Coloured Woodcut by
J. Alphege Brewer*

THE ALPS

By

R. L. G. IRVING

Illustrated from Photographs

LONDON
B. T. BATSFORD LTD.
15 NORTH AUDLEY STREET, W.1
AND AT MALVERN WELLS

By the same author:
The Romance of Mountaineering, 1938

First published, October 1939

MADE AND PRINTED IN GREAT BRITAIN
FOR THE PUBLISHERS, B. T. BATSFORD LTD., LONDON
BY WESTERN PRINTING SERVICES LTD., BRISTOL

AUTHOR'S NOTE

THE Alps is a very big subject; I knew as much when Mr. Batsford asked me to write a text to supplement the pictures he was proposing to collect. I was still more aware of it when I had written it. But, after all, the universe and God are bigger, and I am sure the men who write about them would not claim an exhaustive knowledge of either. The very size of the Alps increases the chance of my having added something of interest to those whose general knowledge of the chain is greater than mine.

It is not these of whom I was thinking when I wrote. Not long ago a young fellow came to tell me he was going to the Alps and asked me what sort of tour I would advise. He went the tour I gave him, and when he came back he said he meant to spend every holiday he could that way. That is the type of person I have had in the back of my mind; and if any man or woman, young or old, is persuaded by this book to visit some part of the Alps with equally good results, will he send me a postcard? It would be the making of a day to read such a card at breakfast. In a few days after writing this note I hope to be in the Alps once more. What I climb when I get there has ceased to matter. It is good for youth to measure its strength with great mountains and it is good for age to know its physical limitations. The Alps can give to the young who climb them and to the old who look at them the knowledge of the things which belong unto their peace.

R. L. G. I.

The Hospice, St. Giles's Hill,
    Winchester.
July 1939.

ACKNOWLEDGMENT

THE Publishers gratefully acknowledge their obligations to the following photographers who have kindly allowed their subjects to be reproduced in this volume:
Baehrendt, L., Merano, 117; Black Star Publishing Co., London, 49, 118; Brassai, Paris, 49; Brewer, J. Alphege, the frontispiece, 1; Brocherell, G., 60; Brütsch, S., 88; Crauffer, 16; Defner, Dr. A., Innsbruck, 118; Ferraris, Pietro, Valtournanche, 86; Feuerstein, Schuls-Tarasp, 32; Fox Photos, Ltd., London, 40; Gabarell, J., Helwil, 62, 65, 110; Geiger, Jules, Flims-Waldhaus, 99; General Photographic Agency, London, 8, 109; Goetz, Emil, Lucerne, 68; Gos, Emile, Lausanne, 64; Guler, R., Thusis, 97; Gyger, E., Adelboden, 66, 71, 75, 79, 89, 90, 108; Hutzli, 22, 24; Italian State Tourist Department, London, 48, 126; Keystone View Co., Ltd., London, 23; Klopfenstein, A., Adelboden, 73, 74, 93; Külley, Dr. G. A., Innsbruck, 116; Meerkämper, E., 21; Mischol, D., Schiers, 17, 82, 113; Myers, Lucien, London, 26; Neumann, G., Munich, 4, 5, 13, 30, 85, 102, 103, 104, 107, 114, 119, 120, 121, 122, 123, 124, 127, 128, 129, 130; Oddoux, Grenoble, 42; Pedrett, A., St. Moritz, 10, 14, 19, 28, 29, 31, 33, 98, 106; Photo X, 46; Pighetti, Cogne, 43; Popper, Paul, London, 2, 7, 34, 36, 58, 67, 69, 72, 80, 81, 83, 84, 87, 91, 92, 94; The Print Society, London, for the frontispiece, 1; Roch, A., Geneva, 6, 59; Roubier, Jean, Paris, 57; Schmaderer, Ludwig, Munich, 27; Schmidbauer, Munich, 77; Schmidt, 78; Schocher, Pontresina, 18, 25, 100; Schönwetter-Elmer, H., Glarus, 112; Skerlep-Fanke, 131; Steiner, Albert, St. Moritz, 3, 9, 11, 12, 15, 76, 96, 105, 111, 115; Swiss Federal Railways, London, 16, 70, 89, 112; Tairraz, Cl., Chamonix, 50, 52, 53, 54, 56; Yvon, Paris, 51.

Nos. 20, 35, 37, 38, 39, 41, 44, 45, 47, 55, 63, 64, 95, and 101 are from the Author's collection.

The Publishers also acknowledge their indebtedness to Mrs. Ruth Matthews for collecting the majority of the photographs.

ERRATA

BESIDE the corrections listed below, the careful reader may notice a few in the case of capital letters, accents, umlauts, etc., and for these indulgence is craved.

Page 5, line 39, *for* "Karamanken" *read* "Karawanken".

,, 7, ,, 23, *for* "Meira" *read* "Maira".

,, 42, ,, 8 and page 44, line 19, *for* "Professor" *read* "Doctor".

,, 64, ,, 44, *for* "1923" *read* "1920".

,, 66, ,, 21, *for* "Courmayer" *read* "Courmayeur".

,, 73, ,, 16, and line 24, *for* "Gstad" *read* "Gstaad".

,, 92, ,, 29, *for* "north" *read* "south".

Figure 36, *for* "Meige" *read* "Meije".

,, 48, *for* "Lillaz" *read* "Lilla".

,, 83, *for* "Fischer" *read* "Fiescher".

,, 119, *for* "Lavoredo" *read* "Lavaredo".

,, 124, *for* "Mandlwand" *read* "Manndlwand".

The older spellings of the endings *thal*, *thor*, *thurm* occur sometimes for *tal*, *tor*, *turm*.

R. L. G. I.

CONTENTS

		Page
AUTHOR'S NOTE	. . . . . .	V
ACKNOWLEDGMENT	. . . . . .	vi
STRUCTURE OF THE ALPS	. . . . .	viii

Chap.

I.	INTRODUCTION	I
	Geology	4
	Flora and Fauna	16
	Climbing	23
II.	THE SOUTH-WESTERN ALPS	36
	Cottian Alps	41
	Dauphiné Alps	45
	Graian Alps	47
III.	THE MONT BLANC RANGE	53
IV.	THE BERNESE ALPS	72
V.	THE PENNINE ALPS	85
VI.	THE CENTRAL ALPS	97
	The Lepontine Alps	97
	The Bernina Group	102
	The Brenta Group	104
VII.	THE EASTERN ALPS, including the DOLOMITES .	109
	The Dolomites	111
	The Julian Alps	114
	INDEX	117

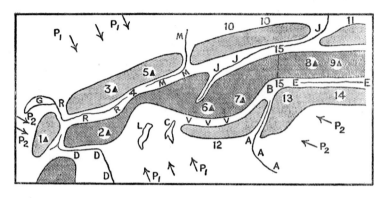

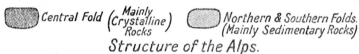

Central Fold (*Mainly Crystalline Rocks*)   Northern & Southern Folds. (*Mainly Sedimentary Rocks*)

Structure of the Alps.

1. Mont Blanc	8. Gross Venediger
2. Monte Rosa	9. Gross Glockner
3. Jungfrau	10. Limestone Alps of Tyrol
4. Region of Furka, Gries and St. Gotthard Passes	11. Salzburg Alps
5. Tödi	12. Bergamesque Alps and Adamello
6. Bernina	13. Dolomites
7. Ortler	14. Carnic Alps
	15. Brenner Pass

P1 P1 line of pressure (nearly N. and S.) producing first folding.
P2 P2 line of pressure (approx. W.N.W. and E.S.E.) producing later folds.

A.A.A. R. Adige (Etsch).
D.D.D. R. Dora Baltea (Val d'Aosta).
E.E. R. Drave   (in upper part)
J.J.J. R. Inn (Engadine in upper part).
M.M.M. R. Rhine (Vorderrhein)
R.R.R. R. Rhone.   V.V.V. R. Adda.

B. Bozen (Bolzano).
C. Lake of Como.
G. Lake of Geneva.
L. Lake Maggiore.

First Stages.

Section across Central Fold (N-S)

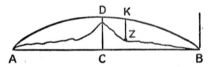

L.L. Sea level. S.S. Top layer of sedimentary rock. C.C. Under layer of crystalline rock. a.a.a. Outer surface of folds before denudation. Black parts are portions of top layer left above sea level after denudation. Note. Core of crystalline rock left exposed above sea level in central fold only. This gives only a very rough idea of what happened, for upheaval and denudation went on together.

A to B (say Pont St. Martin to Visp) CD height of central fold above this level AB must be *at least* 14,000 feet. Height of Zermatt above it about 4,000 feet. Hence ZK (depth of rock that has disappeared) is nearly 10,000 feet, probably much more if we think of what may have disappeared between D and top of crest which at peak of Monte Rosa is 14,000 feet above AB.

viii

2 (*opposite*)
The Matterhorn and Schwarzsee Hotel.

THE ALPS

I

INTRODUCTION

It may be fifty years, it may be five hundred, before every great mountain range in the world has been mapped and photographed, its beauties described, advertised and in some measure destroyed and all its peaks climbed. The limelight of novelty and record-breaking will have ceased to search the Alps and Himalaya with its calculating glare and they will be judged in the light of the fuller knowledge and the more comprehensive view that time inevitably brings. The North face of the Eiger, with its views of daring men hanging alive or dead from its sheer precipices, the last two thousand feet of Everest, which can remove pleasure from every moment except that of turning back, these will have long ago surrendered their news value to other contests in which we love to see the human machine tested to the breaking point. But, if the human race is not utterly different from what it has been and what it is, the Alps will seem to it the best of all ranges in the world, because they have given most and can still give most of beauty, health and liberation of the spirit.

Higher and less accessible mountains in Central Asia or Alaska test men's endurance more severely; they drain his energies rather than restore them; they prove those qualities which an Englishman admires in the bull-dog and a Scotsman in the spider, but continued contact with them seems often to deaden the mental faculties and crush out appreciation under the weight of perpetual discomfort. It is a pleasant fact, particularly true in the case of mountain adventure, that when a man writes of his experiences some weeks or months after they have happened, the hours of discomfort and monotony are veiled in a general sense of satisfaction, and there is also a tendency to transfer to actual moments on the mountain emotions with which his mind has connected them before and after. In a letter or in conversation with intimate friends we are more likely to have the truth and nothing but the truth. This is what Mallory wrote towards the end of his first and most thrilling visit to Everest: "The great mountains give their flashes of beauty; Makalu is indescribably impressive; but on the whole they are disappointing and infinitely less beautiful than the Alps."

I

The Alps are like a good wine sufficiently mellowed, suited to almost every palate; a wine that makes glad the heart and leaves no ill effects, save in a few whose object seems to be to see how much of it they can drink at a sitting. There are mountains higher and further away which provide a wine that is sharper and headier, more potent to affect the legs and mind; and there will always be men who have a craving for such wine. The wine of the Alps keeps well, it is reasonably cheap, and you may drink it either in hilarious company, or with only a few select friends, or in the solitude that is still to be found in at least nine out of ten square miles of the Alps above 6,000 feet.

The hilarious company has taken to choosing its wine iced in the form of winter sports; some of the flavour is lost, but it gives a fine refreshing drink, and that is all that most of this company want. It would be absurd to assure these company-loving folks that it is still very easy in the Alps to avoid the crowd; they love it. And every year the railway, the *téléférique* and the motor-road are pushing further up into the high valleys of the Alps. In so doing they have made access to some of their beauties easier for the lover of solitude as well as for the tourist stream and this stream they have in many places canalized. The Alps are big; even near Chamonix and Zermatt, St. Moritz and Cortina it is not difficult to find unbroken solitude. And when you blaspheme the commercial enterprise which brings some of the noise and hustle of town life into the recesses of the mountains, spare a word of gratitude that it has spared you the long, hot trudge along the valley floor.

So much has been written about the Alps, so thoroughly have they been exploited by avarice and vanity that a man who did not know them might well believe that there is nothing to discover there. Hackneyed, over-run, vulgarised, these are the epithets that have been flung at them. The discovery of the Alps is still to be made by you, if you have not already made it; no one can make it for you. You may not like mountains; then there is no more to be said. But if you do, do not be deterred from visiting the Alps by the fact that thousands have discovered in the past the good things that are there. It is true that excellent maps can be bought and comfortable quarters found which one does not associate with undiscovered lands. The knowledge of what others have done and can safely do has robbed the enterprise of many imagined dangers and difficulties; it has not removed the treasure to be found, and it really has not spoiled the joy of discovering it. If it were a question of benefits that were capable of being measured and were limited in quantity, then it would be only natural to resent having to share them with thousands of others. There are, admittedly, in the Alps, many such benefits that are limited; first ascents of peaks, rare flowers in certain places, corner seats in trains, blankets in huts and so forth; and it must be admitted that men and women are seldom at their best in the competition to obtain them. But unless we are in very bad case, we do not resent in others the possession of health, the opportunity and the power to appreciate beauty or to acquire knowledge of great matters. And it is these things, health, beauty and the knowledge that cannot be conveyed by books, that are the real treasure of the Alps. The supply is inexhaustible. The last is often gained most easily in solitude, and that may still be found in any district of the Alps, though the aeroplane with its horrid drone can banish it temporarily from a larger area than hundreds of train-loads delivered at the valley head. Something will have to be done to keep large portions of the sky and the earth below free from these pests; for pests they can be, even when they do not carry bombs. The more the social life of man develops, the greater will become his need for occasional times of solitude. And it is in solitude, away from all evidences of man's activity and in the presence of forces unseen and mysteriously purposeful that the Alps reveal their nature to us and make us aware of kinship with them.

Sit alone beside the troubled stream of a glacier, with the clouds all round you and the consciousness of silent summits watching behind you and in front; the world of every day may seem very far away. There is a sudden clatter of a stone avalanche falling high up in the mist that dies away in the klok! klok! of the last blocks that come to rest among the boulders down below. The moment comes when a flake of ice in the chaos of the glacier melts to excessive thinness and gives way, letting the block that held it lurch forward and crash into the chasm underneath. You cannot but be conscious of a process going on, a process that has gone on for countless generations and will continue to go on. You may feel reminded of your child-like terror of the dark, a consciousness of powers that lurk unseen. You may picture the final disappearance of the glacier, the final levelling of the peak, both of them annihilated by the relentless forces of decay. And then as you go down across the waste of stones which the diminishing glacier has left below its end, you will find small gems of brilliant colours, forget-me-nots, gentians, ranunculus and many others, and you will remember that it is the melting ice and the crumbling rock that have been built up into this form of beauty; that the process was not one of destruction but of change. It is a pleasant thought, this one of change, the creation of new individuality, new personality by the instrumentality of the old, though it involved the material disappearance of the latter.

And this thought leads on to what is perhaps the most enduring and the happiest of all our thoughts about the Alps; that we too, as we spend our energies and bestow our admiration and affection on them are helping to develop in them a personality, whose influence upon men will grow, affecting and helping to create other personalities. How much more Mont Blanc means to men of this generation than when Saussure visited it in the eighteenth century! Then, it had hardly ceased to be the Mont Maudit, the Accursed Mountain, a name that is still attached to the first conspicuous eminence that rises below the summit on the long north-easterly ridge. Mont Blanc is now a personality with a long history, the subject of many books and innumerable records; we cannot think of Chamonix without it. Materially, it is almost exactly what it was 200 years ago; its personality, like our own, has been made by association with other personalities outside it, by the curiosity and the aspirations it aroused in scientists like Saussure, in poets like Shelley, in many generations of climbers who spent themselves upon it and learned its greatness and the liberality with which it can bestow its gifts.

The separation between the scientific and the sporting interests of a visit to the Alps has widened to an unfortunate degree. Geologists use a language that is as obscure to the ordinary man as that of medicine at its most obscure. In their simplest books they talk of faults and thrustplanes as if they were as familiar as punctures and skidding. It is a pity. A man may be no archeologist and yet like to know something of the history and growth of an old building. There must be many who have not the time or inclination to learn the language of fossils or to read the books of those who pore over them in their glass cases, and who may nevertheless, like to have some picture in their minds of how the snowy ranges of Central Europe were lifted up and sculptured into their present form. The attempt made here to give that picture is brief, sketchy, quite unlearned, but in the main as true as history that is intelligent guesswork can be, till further knowledge modifies it. (See diagrams on p. viii.)

A long time ago, just how many million years ago does not matter to us, a sea extended over the region now covered by

4, 5 Summer and Winter
Contrasts in the Kaiserthal

6 The Grandes Jorasses and the Valais Alps from Mont Blanc

7 The skiers' road to Concordia from the Jungfraujoch

the Alps, and far below its surface the earth was troubled, as things as hot as was the earth always are troubled, by all sorts of stresses and pressures, whose effects on their surfaces appear in bulges, cracks and wrinkles. The solid crust that formed the sea floor consisted of a top layer of what are called sedimentary rocks, so called because they are formed by the sediment, largely composed of the shells of marine creatures, that gradually accumulates at the bottom of the sea. Chalk is a soft form of such rock; dolomite limestone a harder form. This layer of sedimentary rock had been deposited on an older layer of crystalline rock, which generally crystallized to solid form from a liquid state. Granite is a typical rock of this kind, and whether it is in the form of a great peak or a small handhold there is no better rock to look at or to climb.

This crust was heaved up and folded, and the folds rose above the sea. If you are not able to believe in an intelligent purpose at the back of this earth movement, you may at least be grateful for the glorious effects that have resulted from it which have given us the greatest central source of health, of sport and electric power in Europe. Three folds, a central one running roughly east and west, and one on either side of it to north and south are the only ones we need consider. The pressure that squeezed the earth's crust into these folds would, of course, act at right angles to them.

Directly the convex surface of the central fold appeared like the back of a whale above the water, the forces of demolition in the sky, rain, changes of temperature and slow chemical action, got to work upon it, while the sea kept up a constant battering round it. The effect would be to remove a great deal of the crust, especially of the top layer of sedimentary rock, thus exposing the crystalline layer below. This is the beginning of the main chain, whose highest summits, Monte Rosa, the Bernina, and in the Hohe Tauern the Gross Venediger and the Gross Glockner, are of crystalline rock.

The folds to north and south also rose, but not at first so high. They are still well marked in the Eastern Alps; the northern one forms the limestone Alps of North Tyrol and the Salzburg Alps, the southern one the Dolomites, the Carnic, Julian and Karamanken Alps. In these ranges the sedimentary crust almost everywhere overlies the crystalline. In the western part of the chain the southern fold has been almost entirely removed by denudation; the northern fold has given us the Bernese Oberland, where the sedimentary rocks attain their highest elevation in the Eiger, which just passes 13,000 feet;

the other summits over this height are crystalline, the upper layer having been entirely worn away.

Consider now what happened to the central fold after it was exposed to the forces of the air. Rain fell, and ran down the slopes, scooping out valleys to north and south. These valley torrents would become more and more powerful agents of demolition as the central range was raised higher by intensified folding. They would flow north and south till they came up against the folds on either side of the chain; they would then have to flow east or west along the trough of the fold. You can still see them doing this in parts. It is easy to follow the general line of the northern trough on any map that shows the physical features well. You can mark it very clearly in the long, nearly straight stretch of the Rhone valley from the Furka to Martigny. West of Martigny later upheavals have introduced complications. The Swiss Val Ferret and the Italian Val Ferret may be a continuation of the trough. Beyond this, the fold may continue in stretches of the Isère valley. East of the Furka the upper Rhine follows the same great trough to Chur, and the Inn runs in it for a long way east of Landeck. If the earth's crust had been left in peace after this first folding and upheaval the structure of the Alps would have been comparatively simple. It was not so by any means. A second upheaval and folding took place. The folds run in a different direction, north-north-east to south-south-west. The Lake of Garda and the upper Adige lie in one of these folds and this fold is probably seen again in the Brenner Pass; the Inn below Samaden probably runs in another; in the west this new folding may account for the approximate north and south direction of the main chain south of the Dauphiné Alps.

The new uplifting of the crust was particularly marked in the Bernese Oberland, in the Mont Blanc chain and in the Central Alps of Dauphiné, these last summits being pushed up through the upper sedimentary strata. And with this uplifting occurred a violent folding and frequent dislocation of the crust in the northern parts of the Alps, possibly due to their being pressed against a solid mass of older crystalline rock in the north-west. Here is one fact that will give you some idea of the importance of this upheaval and of the time that must have elapsed since the birth of the main chain. The Rigi is nearly 6,000 feet high and it is composed of a pebbly mass that was deposited in a sort of huge delta where the rivers from the main chain arrived at or near sea-level.

You can imagine the complications such new folding and

8 A Bergschrund near
   the Jungfraujoch

9 On Piz Palu : a
   Snow Cornice

[Note the black dots of climbers in these views.]

10 Lurching Séracs

11 A "Dry" Glacier

upheaval would produce! Think of what the sea is like under the influence of a wind that blows strongly across a heavy swell left by a previous storm, or the effect upon the folds of the bed-clothes by a slight turn of the body! The later upheaval of the Mont Blanc range and of the Dauphiné Alps has played strange tricks with the watersheds in those districts, so that the Dora Baltea, born in the glaciers of Mont Blanc, cuts right through the central crystalline chain and runs into the Po and the Adriatic.

And beside all these complications due to movements below the crust there are others of unexpected character above it, due to the excessive activity of running water as an excavator. The Rhone valley affords a very clear example. As we said above, the Rhone follows the natural trough originally made for it from its source to Martigny. Why does it suddenly there make a turn sharper than a right angle and flow north? Because a stream flowing down the northern slopes at the west end of the Bernese Oberland chain cut through that chain and tapped the drainage of the upper Rhone valley. There are many other cases of this behaviour.

A somewhat similar example is that seen at the Maloja. The nearly level valley running up from St. Moritz once continued much further to the south. But the more rapid stream in the Val Meira, which we see far below us from the Maloja pass, ate its way back and cut off the head of the high flat valley, so that the Forno glacier now drains into the southern stream instead of north. It needs no expert knowledge to recognize other instances of this rough treatment of the old by younger torrents perpetually hurrying to get somewhere.

Enough has been said to give some indication of how the Alps arose and took shape. The rest of the complicated story is left to the reader, that he may treat it as he likes; it may have no interest whatever for him or it may offer a fine field for intelligent speculation.

In the detailed shaping of the peaks and valleys water, ice and disintegration due to changes of temperature or chemical action have all played a part. Wordy battles have been waged over the relative importance of these agents. Water wins. Glaciers were at one time credited with extraordinary powers of excavation, plucking out rocks from faces like expert dentists and gouging out huge lakes. As agents of demolition they are now *démodés*, capable of little beyond abrasion of the surface—and of scratching. Stones of various sizes get fixed in the ice at the sides and bottom of the ice and the pressure of the enorm-ous mass against the rocky bed of the glacier as it moves down causes these stones to cut grooves which are called striation marks. The general effect of the passage of the glacier is like that of a polishing cloth or pad, to smooth the surface; if, however, a bit of grit or glass gets on to your pad, striation of the surface is produced. As rubbish collectors glaciers are very effective. There is no need for the mountains to wait till a cart comes down the road to get rid of their litter, consisting of stones and mud detached by frost or rain. The whole road below them moves; they have only to roll the stuff on to it and the glacier tips it all at the road end, where it is gradually converted into an Alpine garden. These tips are for a time unsightly, and may extend for many miles, but often they have become so completely covered up with pleasant grass and flowers that nothing remains to show the casual visitor they have been tips except one or two specially large discarded rocks so delicately balanced on an edge that no transport less careful than that of ice could have left them where they are. There are fragments on the slopes of the Jura as well as on the sides of the Rhone valley between Martigny and the Lake of Geneva, which have been thrown down by the Mont Blanc range and transported by the Rhone glacier when it occupied the whole of the valley that bears its name and reached to the Jura.

A heavy covering of snow is really a very beneficent oppressor of what is beneath, compared with the wastage that occurs from free exposure to the activities of air and water. You often find in the Alps high valleys, nearly level, with a steep drop into the main valley, so steep as to produce a fine waterfall or more than one. Saas Fee is in such a high side valley; the Almagellalp a little higher up on the opposite side of the main Saas valley, is an even better example. How have these valleys been shaped? Perhaps, in a colder period of Europe's early history, these valleys were filled with snow; the water from melting snow seeps into the ground and has no excavating power, while in the main valley lower down, the snow might disappear for a considerable part of the year and excavation would go on there, cutting down the floor of the valley further and further below that of the upper side valleys. But here, we are on controversial ground and had better leave it.

Water has been the chief agent in shaping the valleys, and what a prodigious work it has been! Go back for a moment to that great convex fold in the earth's crust which was the beginning of the main chain. The distance in a straight line on the map due north from the summit of Monte Rosa to Visp at the bottom of the Rhone Valley is about twenty-six miles. You may regard the top of the fold there as forming a wide-splayed arch with a span of about fifty miles and clearing Monte Rosa, we cannot say by how much, but certainly clearing it. The point where Zermatt now is, is three times as far from the northern end of the arch as from the middle so that the depth of the arch there would be almost as great as in the centre. The difference of height between Zermatt and Monte Rosa is nearly 10,000 feet; which means that the depth of rock excavated in order to bring the valley level down to Zermatt cannot have been much less than that, and may have been more. When one thinks of the Visp flowing year after year at apparently just the same level below the meadows and the chalets by its banks, near Zermatt, the time that must have been required to remove these thousands of feet of rock and leave the Matterhorn in its present glorious isolation is an almost astronomical number of years. It is not hurried work.

The shaping of the Alps is still going on, but so little perceptible change happens in a life-time that the interest of the process lies in a distant, often problematical past. The clothing of the Alps, their preparation and adornment for the reception of visitors is a very present interest. This is entirely in the hands of the earth's outside department, the clouds, the sunshine and the air.

White is always becoming to mountains; it is worn at all seasons by the best peaks. For the tall, those above 10,000 feet, it is *de rigueur*, even in summer. Very long ago the Alps realized the joys of sunbathing. The fashion of leaving considerable portions of the body bare in the hottest months is very old, as old as the hills! Roughly speaking, it never rains, it only snows, above 8,000 feet. At the beginning of a wet period rain may fall at greater heights, but before the weather improves it will have turned to snow, often much below 8,000 feet even in July and August. The Matterhorn is a good recorder of the weather fashions of the year. If it has been a fine season, the east face, the one that faces you as you go up to the Gornergrat from Zermatt, will be bare, hardly anything but a shoulder-strap or the remnant of one left upon it. And once the peak has bared itself like this, it will very quickly throw off any but a heavy snowfall, just keeping the white on long enough, when the clouds clear, to show you how attractive it can be. If there has been no long period of sunny, warm weather, only enough warmth to turn the snow to ice, the peak may never get into good condition for climbing. Height, as well as weather, has a great effect on the rate of disappearance of snow or ice. The greater cold high up not only delays melting, but a much larger proportion of what is melted is turned to ice at night.

There are endless variations in the thickness, the extent and the condition of the snow-covering of the Alps. Your enjoyment and your safety may depend upon your knowledge and your correct anticipation of how much snow there is, and what it is like. Its effect on rock-peaks is seldom appreciated by the inexperienced, and the guide-books describe ascents of them as if the tourist agencies had seen to it that they were in good, dry, favourable conditions. Snow introduces fresh dangers from avalanches and, in the melting stage, from stone-falls; it conceals holds, it makes the rocks cold, and a veneer of ice will make them unbelievably slippery, even for nailed boots. Nor is it only rock-peaks that are affected. The approach to most high passes and most high peaks is by a glacier and the slopes that rise above it. Glaciers are wild, fascinating, lovely things; and like other things of that nature they need knowing; they are most changeable, never the same from day to day or even from hour to hour. They have, however, certain features in common. They must all be fed from a basin high up above the snow line. The typical form of this basin is a comparatively level snowfield with steep walls of varying height surrounding it.

The word _névé_ is loosely used to describe either the upper snowfield itself or the substance that is formed by continual melting, freezing and pressure as snow passes into ice at high altitudes. On the steep faces that rise from the snowfield to the crest of the high rim enclosing it you may get bare rock, ice, snow or _névé_, according to aspect, height above sea level or weather. Very high up, especially on the upper slopes of Mont Blanc, where the temperature can hardly ever be above the freezing point below the surface, you find _névé_ that is hard and tough, in which the pick of the axe sticks; generally, however, on steep places that are not bare rock, you will find either snow or ice that the pick will fracture; quite often you have to clear away an inviting and treacherous covering of the former and hack out the slow, grudging, but trustworthy support of the latter.

In summer the lower glacier moves quicker than in winter and the surface of the upper snowfield sinks by melting faster than it is raised by falls of snow upon it. Consequently it tends to draw away from the enclosing walls of rock and leaves a gap between them and itself. Late in a fine summer this gap may be a chasm whose upper overhanging lip is twenty feet above the lower lip. The gap is clearly shown in photographs of

12 The Rigi

13 The Grossglockner
and the Pasterze
Glacier

14 Hanging On to a Rock Wall

high glacier basins; it is called the *Bergschrund* or *rimaie*. I do not think the purist who objects to calling ridges *arêtes* and gullies *couloirs* can give us a good English equivalent for *névé* or *Bergschrund*.

In these high snowfields you are at the heart of the Alps. Some of them are expanses so wide and open that great peaks seem only to mark their limits and not to dominate them. The head of the Grenz Glacier is one. As you enter that great horseshoe, the Lyskamm presents an imposing wall on your right, while on your left, some way inside the entrance, the wall of Monte Rosa offers a grand climb up the Crestone Rey to the highest point, the Dufour-Spitz; but all the back of the horseshoe is a chain of minor points, the gaps between which hardly rise above the snowfield on which you stand. It gives you a feeling of immensity and of being lifted up, isolated from the world by height alone. Within an hour or two of dawn, there will be no shadow but your own to break the sheet of dazzling whiteness; it is a revelation of the splendour of light and the greatness of the upper world. If there are other parties there, the presence of those tiny objects across the expanse of snow will enhance the impression of greatness.

There are other gathering grounds of snow where you are conscious, above all else, of seclusion, of intimacy with what has personality as well as greatness. It is not a great reception room, it is a private sanctum you are in. The presence of another party here, even the tracks they may have left, diminishes the impression of privileged intimacy. It is in these less famous, secluded recesses of the Alps that you will most easily discover your own special sanctum where the Alps will murmur their secrets to you. Much depends upon the day, the hour, your own mood. There is a bay of the upper Géant Glacier, under the Tour Ronde and the Mont Maudit; there is a small snowfield under the Lyskamm on the Italian side; another above Arolla under the Douves Blanches; and there is the Ciardoney Glacier in the Cogne district, a long way from any inn or hut. These are the sort of places where you may expect to find the mountains most communicative. For me the time has most often been early morning when the air is calm and the sky serene. The stillness, the absolute purity of the snowy floor, the lovely curves of the steepening walls that rise from it, the beauties that the winds and frosts have hung upon them, the golden light that plays among their corniced crests; to be with these is to be in the bosom of the Alps. And there is no danger shared, no victory won, that can bind you to a friend so fast as the unuttered thought that fills your mind and his: "It is good for us to be here."

The age and thickness of the carpet most recently laid upon these upper snowfields is an important matter for those who walk upon it. A freshly fallen one will not support the foot at all, and it will reflect fierce, burning rays into your eyes and skin. After a single fine day and night, it will be crusted, but insufficiently to bear you; it will make large demands on your strength and patience. After two or three fine days and nights it will offer you a hard surface perfect for walking till the sun has melted the crust; but even if there are not others' tracks to help, you will by then be across the snowfields or descending them; it is nothing to sink into it, provided you do not do it over a crevasse. Aspect and altitude have great effect. A single day on sunny slopes at 9,000 feet will cure the troubles brought by a fall of snow, when it may need four or five to do it on sunless slopes or at 14,000 feet.

Below its high gathering-ground the glacier is pushed through a valley. If the bed of the glacier steepens, crevasses are likely to occur at the bend-over; at the foot of a steep portion where the descending ice joins the lower ice and presses on it there is likely to be an uncrevassed stretch. If the steepness occurs over the whole width of the glacier the result may be a chaos of shattered, tumbling ice that is quite impassable and must be turned by the slopes on one side or other. If these slopes are steep, masses of snow slide off them on the margin of the glacier, and in consequence an easy way is found more often at the sides than in the middle of a glacier where it descends steeply between high mountain walls.

Most glaciers end in a steep tongue of bare ice down which stones are constantly falling. In the case of big glaciers it is generally far below the line of perpetual snow. In August you may expect a glacier to be bare of snow up to at least 9,000 feet and steep sunny portions may be bare much higher. On a fine summer afternoon such a glacier if it is uncrevassed has streams of water flowing all over it, but it is nevertheless known as "dry" glacier, if it is bare of snow. The surface may be clean and from a distance look gleaming white if it comes from fields of snow and is not shut in between rocky slopes. The Bossons Glacier comes down below 4,000 feet into the valley of Chamonix, and is still clean and white. The Miage Glacier on the Italian side flows for a long way below steep rocky slopes that pour their litter on to it; and so it is a river of stones to look at rather than one of ice, though the ice soon betrays its slippery character when you tread the stones that overlie it.

The Oberland glaciers win the prize for size, though the peaks are not quite so high as those we see from them on the other side of the Rhone Valley, stretching from the Weisshorn to Mont Blanc. My experience of Oberland weather convinces me that the glaciers there are better fed. Glaciers are very dependent on their food; they stand warmth much better than starvation. In New Zealand for example, though the climate is at least as warm as that of Switzerland, the glaciers come down much lower because of the fine amount of snow that they requisition from the sea. In the Southern Andes, on the other hand, in spite of the horrible cold that chills the climber there and the superiority in height over the Alps, the glaciers are insignificant.

The Great Aletsch Glacier is the biggest, longest ice-stream in the Alps; it is about sixteen miles long. If you descend on to it from the Belalp or the Riederalp and walk up to the Lötschen-lücke or the Jungfraujoch, either of which might be regarded as its head, you will find it a respectable day's walk; quite long enough to convince you that a glacier in the Alps is a big and wonderful thing; there is no need to go to the Karakoram Himalaya to find that out.

The glaciers in the main chain between the Chamonix valley and the Saas valley are nearly as big. The last big glacier towards the east is the Pasterze Glacier on the Gross Glockner. The Dolomites are not high enough to possess gathering grounds for glacier streams; the highest, the Marmolata, which just passes 11,000 feet, has a mantle of snow cast over what all Dolomite enthusiasts would regard as the least honourable portions of its form. Striking and wonderful as they are, these fantastic towers lack the special nobility which their height above the snow line confers upon the higher summits of the Alps; beside these taller, serener figures of the alpine scene, the Dolomites are passionate contortionists.

Alpine glaciers are subject to considerable variations in size. Great heaps of stones below the present lower limits of the ice, which time has not yet converted into green slopes, show their diminution in the last few generations of men. Their admirers may take heart from the knowledge that in the Middle Ages they were less extensive than at the present time. The years 1850–78 were a period of rapid diminution; since then there have been shorter periods of variation, diminution being on the whole in excess of slight increases. The variation which

4

begins in the gathering ground is not shown till some time later at the lower end. I noticed an interesting example of this in the Brenva Glacier on the Italian side of Mont Blanc. In 1923 an enormous mass of rock came away from the Peuteret ridge not far below the top of the mountain. It must have weighed about eight million tons and it fell on to the glacier. Ice is elastic and must have acted something like a pillow; if punched in one place it bulges in another. A punch with eight million tons behind it is not a gentle one, even for a glacier, and in a year or two the wall of ice in which the glacier ended began to advance and threaten to obliterate the small restaurant that stood at what had been thought a safe distance away. Fortunately the advance stopped just in time.

In winter, visitors to the Alps expect to find them completely clad in a thick covering of snow down to 3,000 feet, which is about the lowest altitude at which a place can claim to call itself an Alpine resort. From the middle of January to the middle of March this expectation will generally be fulfilled. Before that time it may be unfulfilled up to a much higher level. At the end of December things can look black for the skier; bare black rocks, bare black trees and even bare black earth confront him under the moon, instead of the silvery, frost-bound landscape of his dreams. The further east he goes the more likely he is to find plenty of snow at the doubtful level at this time.

Winter visitors to the Alps are more inclined than others to be guided in their choice of place by advertisements or by the opinions of others, whose ideas of enjoyment may be different from their own. It is interesting and it may prevent disappointment to let an intelligent study of the map assist your choice. Altitude and aspect are the important things, both in the place itself and in the neighbouring slopes to which you will look for sport. The map will give you a very good idea of the amount of sunshine, the angle of the slopes, the likelihood of crust, the views you may enjoy; it can tell you nothing of the social attractions or the disturbances to peace which the invading crowd brings with it.

Seventy years ago Mr. A. W. Moore and his friends discovered the pleasures of winter expeditions in a fine spell of weather in the Alps. Skis have done much to solve the problem of crossing long stretches of deep powdery snow without excessive toil; and it is as an ally, not a rival to the climber's hopes, that the ski should be regarded. There is one sort of slope where the human tortoise on foot has an advantage in security over the human hare on skis; the steep slope where snow lies loosely on ice or hard old snow. The foot will go through to the firm support below, the ski does not, and may push the loose snow down, causing a slip or an avalanche. If the consequences of either of these would be serious, it is usually better to go straight up or down such slopes on foot. If the loose top layer is thin steps can be cut.

April has not yet obtained the recognition it deserves for visiting the Alps. Hotel activity is then at its lowest; there is little to attract the more gregarious members of our race. A limited number of good skiers know that glacier tours can be specially delightful at this time; the days are long, the sun glorious, the crevasses nicely filled. Modern civilization, pursuing its ideal of physical comfort, is rapidly providing lifts in the shape of *téléfériques* and railways like those of the Gornergrat and Jungfrau to transport the visitor to the point where the ski ceases to be a burden and becomes a blessing.

If not an expert skier, you may be a ruminant. The human ruminant differs from the bovine variety in being non-gregarious; he likes to chew the cud, that is to say, to assimilate beauty, alone or in the company of intimates. For the ruminant the southern valleys of the Alps, particularly those that open near the Mediterranean may be a paradise in spring. Skiers are warned off by large, bare patches on southern slopes and by the prevalence of snow that is either crusted or so soggy that it will let even his seven-foot boots sink far below the surface. Sunny slopes may be bare up to 7,000 feet, but you cannot count on this. I have arrived at San Dalmazzo di Tenda in the Maritime Alps when such conditions prevailed, and within forty-eight hours everything was under a foot of snow to a point far below the village, which is just above 2,000 feet. A few days later I was able to walk up to the top of the Roccia del Abisso, a marvellous view-point, over 9,000 feet high, up a south-facing rib, almost without a single step in really heavy snow. Another advantage of ascending this point and other points along the Franco-Italian frontier in early spring is that you are less likely to be shot, but I must refer to that again in the section dealing with the western Alps.

So much for the snow the Alps wear for the delight and sport of men; it is the dress that marks their eminence. Below it are the green pasture, the alp, the verdant zone between the forest and the regions of perpetual snow, which gives its name to the whole range and sets the Alps as a pleasure-ground above all other ranges in the world. Among great mountains, if we look up from the valley-depths to the last serrated ridges, we can appreciate their grandeur, their wild beauty; it is on the green alp that we feel their bounty. Here everything reminds us what generous givers mountains are. Above us now are the slopes up which we ploughed or hewed our way; against the sky the final ridge with its towers, tiny from here but up there huge and forbidding, where every muscle of our bodies strove for success, the success that is now sweetened by the languor in our limbs, the summit itself where effort ceased, the body no longer spending but receiving, the mind no longer questioning, sure that it has found a way that leads to the source of truth and beauty. Round the small chalet, close at hand now, where we know the path begins, the cows are gathering at milking time. By rolling over we can dip our fingers or our faces in the streamlet that is hurrying to convey to lower levels all the blessings that fresh water brings. And all about us are the flowers!

The twentieth century has certainly discovered in the Alps a flower garden—for very many people unfortunately, a garden they can rob. Hundreds of motorists drone up to the high pastures and carry off great bunches of flowers of all sorts, the rarest being specially prized, forgetting that they are thereby robbing those that follow them of some of the beauty they have come to see. It is a pity, for compared with the first thrill of seeing the flower growing in its natural setting, the satisfaction the plunderer gets from seeing it die in the concentration camp in his own room must be very small. To take a few blooms for those who have no chance of seeing their beauty otherwise is a different matter; I think the bulk of the flowers that are now taken would be left unpicked, if this were the only intention of the pickers. Collectors who dig up whole plants are worse offenders. There is a law in Switzerland against the practice, but it must be very often broken with impunity. Why not be content with taking the seed or buying it? it costs little and raising from seed is an excellent way of propagating most alpine plants.

There is this immense advantage the Alps possess over flatter places rich in flowers; the flowering season is at different times at different heights. Many flowers have a wide range of height and may be found in bloom at any time from April to August. And let us be thankful that those that are among the first in beauty have little of the commercial value that depends on rarity. The big blue trumpets of the acaulis gentian open to the sun in April up to 3,000 feet and are still opening to it in thousands above 6,000 feet in July; it is at home on most

15 *Arenaria Grandiflora*

16 (*overleaf*)
     Spring Crocus on the Wiesener Alp near Davos

(17) Chamois Hunter . . .   (18) Chamois and . . .

(19) Bouquetins

Alpine meadows. The *verna* displays its sapphire stars in April too, but it is a better climber than acaulis; you may find it far above the pastures in August. There is also a wide range in the period of blooming at the same altitude. The small rhododendrons *ferrugineum* and *hirsutum*, commonly known as *alpenrose*, are in blossom in June near Le Lautaret, and I have seen the former in bloom near the Grimsel at the same altitude in September—which supports the view that the Grimsel is the worst place for weather in the Alps. That does not mean it will not be fine there, if it is fine everywhere else!

The flower display in August depends much on the type of season. Less spring snow than usual and a fine June mean fewer blooms and fewer uncut pastures. If June and July have been bad months for the climber, there will be compensation for the flower-lover; the sulphur anemone may have waited for you, if you could not get to the Alps before August. This flower knows the best rock and you will find it on granite, not on limestone. There is a grassy hollow within half an hour's walk of a well-known hotel in the Pennines, where I have sat surrounded by scores of these large primrose-yellow stars. Generally you must be there in the first half of July, and early in the day if you are near a popular centre. I once saw three blooms on one of the less frequented paths on the Brévent above Chamonix; needless to say, they had disappeared when I came back in the afternoon.

This lust for possession even shows itself in the way people talk of Alpine flowers; they must have the best for themselves. "You should have been here at the beginning of the month when we came; the pastures then were simply covered", or, "The flowers are nothing here; you should see them in the Tyrol", etc. etc. The fact is that the Alps can gratify all tastes. If you want profusion with sheets of colour, the limestone ranges, especially those of the Eastern Alps are the best place. If you go late in June to pastures there, say near the Pordoi Pass, you will be able to say that for colour in the mass there is nothing in the Western and Central Alps to rival them. In this lavish display you lose something of the quality there is in independent colonies of plants. There is a different thrill, a less sensuous thrill, in turning a corner of rock on a high ridge and finding a small cluster of gentians or *ranunculus glacialis*, ethereal things that seem to live on nothing but snow and air and sunshine and make you feel as if you had broken in upon them in the middle of a song. Both of these are common enough to escape the collector's claw and avoid annihilation except in close proximity to frequented roads. Nor can they be easy to cultivate at home. The combination of sunshine and of cold running water at the roots, and the protection of the snow for two thirds of the year, must play a great part in giving this ranunculus its pearly complexion varying from ivory to pink, and these conditions are difficult to ensure for ordinary folks in Britain. There is little danger that either of these two lovely flowers will disappear. I am not so sure if that can be said about the rarer gem, *eritrichium nanum*; this plant is almost certainly doomed to die when transplanted. But it is one of the most precious trophies to bring and show your friends, and it is so beautiful that the temptation to gather it is great. I shall not forget the first time I saw it. I was climbing with a friend along a previously unvisited ridge between 10,000 and 11,000 feet in the Eastern Graian Alps, when we saw on a broad ledge of rock a wonderful blue cushion, which closer examination showed to be a plant with small green woolly leaves completely covered with almost stalkless blooms like forget-me-nots but of a much more vivid blue. There were other plants of it on the rocks near. It was my twelfth visit to the Alps and the previous ones had not been idly spent, so I think it is right to describe this plant as rather rare. I have seen it several times since, but never much, if at all, below 10,000 feet, and I have never seen any plant of it to come near the first; the next best was on the Gran Paradiso when we had strayed from the usual route.

Of the meadow flowers, the big blue alpine *aquilegia* is second to none. It is not common. You can find it within half an hour's walk of Le Lautaret on a slope facing north-west and without ascending or descending 200 feet from the Col. The only reward I ask for the information is that you should leave it as you find it.

It is a misfortune that the flower collector should have to leave the Alps the poorer for the loss of what he takes from them. The acquisitive instinct is strong in us and it is by no means in abeyance because we are on holiday, spending money instead of trying to earn it; but in nearly every other case the good things we take home from the mountains are of such a nature and are drawn from such inexhaustible sources of supply that we leave them not a whit the poorer or less able to benefit those who follow us there. The climber returns with a score of peaks or passes in his bag; yet they are still there, for you and me to climb, as high and challenging, as beautiful and as full of possible adventure as before; they are no man's exclusive possession.

We are still a long way in Britain from being able to say that all have free access to what is wildest and most beautiful in it. In the High Alps you will find notices on your way that invite you to halt and eat or drink, you will find none that tell you trespassers will be prosecuted. No keeper or owner will warn you off the mountain, courteously or otherwise, for the Alps are not a sportsman's paradise, if by sportsman is meant a man who visits mountains in order to kill what he finds upon them. Chamois-shooting is restricted to a fortnight in September in the Swiss Alps and there are extensive areas in which no shooting is allowed at all. The result is that even in the neighbourhood of crowded centres chamois are not uncommon. There is a national preserve of this kind on the east side of the Roseg valley near Pontresina and I saw a whole troop of chamois crossing the stream close to the Roseg restaurant while I was having an early breakfast there. The closest I have ever been to a wild chamois was on the Col de Seilon, which is between Arolla and Mauvoisin in the Val de Bagnes. The wind must have prevented the animal from scenting us, for it suddenly appeared almost on top of us and nearly upset our spread-out luncheon as it bounded off down the slopes on the Mauvoisin side.

The bouquetin too is not only holding its own, but is being acclimatised in other districts beside that which was the royal preserve of the King of Italy near Cogne. It is a fine powerful beast, bigger than a chamois, with grand curving horns about a foot and a half in length. It is a member of the goat tribe and is very similar to, though not quite the same as the ibex of other ranges. The chamois is a species of antelope, not a goat. A peasant in a high chalet near Cogne told me how he had once shot a bouquetin in the King's preserve and had almost got it across the bridge near Cogne that forms the boundary when the King's keepers caught him and he was fined 500 lire—pre-War lire too, a heavy penalty for a man whose total income was probably no more.

Marmots are jolly little fellows in thick, fur coats, about the size of a rabbit; you will find them all over the Alps in places covered by a chaos of great fallen rocks, whose crevices afford admirable sheltered quarters, inaccessible to larger beasts. The traditional advice given in a marmot nursery is the opposite of that given to small boys: "Little marmots should be heard and not seen." You will not go through much rock-strewn ground at 7,000 or 8,000 feet in the Alps without hearing the loud shrill whistle of the marmot on sentry duty. If you are

lucky you may see him sunning his dark brown body on a
prominent rock before he scuttles off after uttering his warning
cry at your approach. Marmots are not fresh air fanatics; they
believe in warmth and comfort first. As winter approaches the
family puts a good thick lining of dry grass over its rocky bur-
row; then it stops up the entrance with a thick wad of the same
material and goes to sleep for months, eating nothing and
hardly breathing at all, while the snow lays a covering of some
feet in thickness overhead.

A beast whose slaughter would have secured immortality
for the lucky sportsman and headlines for a week in every
European newspaper is the dragon. Unfortunately the genus
draco disappeared in the eighteenth century, or rather was
exterminated by scepticism. Among the few traces it has left
is a stone which was called a *draconita* or dragon stone, now
in a museum at Lucerne. You can judge of the rarity of
such a trophy by the conditions necessary for obtaining it.
You had to find your dragon asleep, scatter soporific herbs
about him and then cut the stone out of his head without
waking him. In this particular case the stone was dropped by
a flying dragon and picked up by a peasant who was passing
near! Another piece of evidence which we must hesitate to
disbelieve, for it was preserved in a public notice hung up in a
church in Lucerne, tells us how a man passed some of the winter
months with two dragons in a cavernous pit into which he
had fallen. He owed his salvation to an unwonted amiability
on their part, which was either natural or induced by his
fervent appeals to the Virgin Mary. He escaped when the period
of hibernation was over by holding on to the dragons' tails.

Another extinct creature, less terrifying to the imagination
than a dragon but a greater actual danger to young livestock,
was the lammergeier, the bearded vulture of the Alps. Perhaps
it really did occasionally do something to justify its wide-
spread reputation as a baby-snatcher! According to Mr. Coolidge
—and many men have proved the unwisdom of doubting anything he said—the last lammergeier, known as "the old woman",
had an eyrie on the Hohgleifen above Kippel in the Lötschental.
Her mate was shot in 1862, but she went on living for a quarter
of a century, taking regular toll of the cats in the valley till in
1887 she was found dead beside a poisoned fox.

There are, however, other birds to be seen in the Alps,
more interesting, if less notorious than the lammergeier. It is
fascinating to watch a buzzard or an eagle using the upward
current that blows up a great precipice on a fine day as a lift,

(20) Mountain Sheep, (21) Marmot, and (22) Young Eagles in the Eyrie

23 Sheep in the Langkofel in the Dolomites

24 Heavily laden: gear for the upper
huts

circling round to keep within it and soaring up on motionless, outstretched wings.

If you hear a noise like the grunt of an animal where no animal is likely to be, it is probably a ptarmigan. With their speckled dark and white plumage they are not very easy to see against a background of snow and rock till they begin to walk away.

Among the smaller birds seen in the neighbourhood of the summer snow-line the snow-finches are the most strikingly beautiful. A flock of these will evoke a cry of startled delight as they dart past; the white feathers of their plumage flash like sunlit snow against the face of dark rock, and the next moment the black feathers are outlining the flying forms against the white background of the snow itself. The red-winged wall-creeper is another bird that is beautiful in form and most interesting to watch. The chamois has got a pretty good foothold on steep rocks; I remember watching with admiration and envy a couple of them walking up a smooth steep slab near the Col de l'Herbetet with ease and confidence. But the wall-creeper is in a higher class altogether; he shows how to climb absolutely vertical rocks without any artificial aids whatever and eat his luncheon as he does it, holding on with a single wonderful, backward-pointing toe and restoring the balance or relieving the strain from time to time by half opening his wings.

These beasts and birds of the High Alps—and I hope you will agree to add the flowers—are for the observer rather than the collector. There are, however, types of collectors, on whose activities no restrictions are imposed either by authority or by the censorious, and the photographer is one of these. He may take home hundreds of pictures to be a recurring source of pleasure and make no subsequent visitor the poorer. For the artist in oils and water-colours the Alps are a less happy hunting-ground. It is their glory, not their shame, though I have heard the Alps disparaged by those whose culture has led them to look at nature through a picture frame. Two of the most impressive qualities of an Alpine peak are its immense size and the glory of light upon it, and both are almost impossible to represent on a portable canvas. You cannot get the dynamic, quivering power of sunlight on the upper snows, the brightness that will make the whitest paint on a wall look dark, nor can you convey the real effect of a great mountain's size upon a flat surface a few feet square; you might as well attempt to put Polyphemus adequately on a postage stamp. For a

5

Ulysses, who had met him, a photograph which contained the details that would help his recollection might recall the monster. And so it is with Alpine photographs; to a person who does not know the Alps they suggest little of the real Alps. I know this is so, for more than once a glacier nearly half a mile wide in a fine photograph of the Aletschhorn on the walls of my study has been mistaken seriously for a road! The colour artist or the etcher has to leave out so much that helps to suggest size. A skilfully applied patch of dark blue may indicate a hollow in the mountain side; there is nothing to tell you it is a huge green basin where a village may be hidden and hundreds of cattle feed.

The lantern slide, with its brilliant illumination, approaches more nearly than any other form of reproduction to the actual effect of light among snow mountains, but even the slide with all its wealth of detail says only a small fraction of the truth to the person who has no intimate knowledge of the reality. The tiny black excrescence on the ridge cannot convey to him the frowning tower whose sheer walls presented the climber with a choice of extremely difficult routes; the shadow on the wall of snow gives little idea of the great cornice it implies above; the dark line across the bottom of the slopes hardly suggests a chasm with pendant icicles, wonderful to look at and in most places impossible to pass. You cannot get the Alps at second hand; they are a perpetual warning against any attempt to put our limited interpretation on what is much greater than man's work and which has a message that each individual must discover for himself. The Alps are not a subject for art, they are themselves examples of an art which we have only begun to understand. The photographs we bring back are reminders of those masterpieces, just as are the post cards and photographs people bring back from the galleries of Florence or The Hague.

The photographer must be careful to choose for his efforts those sites and aspects of the Alps which offer the best possibilities. The northern side is better than the southern. There the Alps present to him their snowy faces, and these are what give special beauty and character to his pictures, though they may be less attractive to the climber, who is exceptional if he does not prefer rock to snow and ice. In the great watershed that runs across the south of Switzerland from west to east, the northern faces of the Grand Combin, the Rimpfischhorn and Strahlhorn, the three great peaks of the Bernina, Scersen and Roseg are far more varied and beautiful than the bare rocky walls by which they are cut off on the south. Many of the finest peaks, the Dent Blanche, the Weisshorn, the Mischabel peaks and the Weissmies-Fletschhorn ridge lie wholly north of the watershed.

Another point to remember is that the sun will never be directly behind you as you look at the peaks from any point north of them, and every photographer knows that the best lighting effects cannot be obtained with the sun behind him. Some of the best view-points are to be found on the shelves conveniently provided in the Alps that run parallel to the big valleys at a great height above them. From such a shelf the peaks opposite rise to their full height and are seen without undue foreshortening, and if the height of the shelf is in the neighbourhood of 6,000 feet, the trees will have begun to thin out and you will get good foregrounds, which is very difficult on a slope that falls straight away below you. Here are a few among the many shelves of this kind in which the Alps have been extraordinarily generous.

First of all, the famous shelf that runs along the slopes of the Aiguilles Rouges above the valley of Chamonix. For two hours you may walk on a good path, keeping always close to the upper tree limit, where familiarity only increases the enjoyment without diminishing the wonder of the views of the Mont Blanc Range that succeed one another as you come opposite the ice-filled valleys that lead into its recesses. And in Mont Blanc itself you have the one commanding peak that is essential to perfection in a mountain view. In its unchallenged height its naked strength, in the purity and brilliance of the snows that give it rank and grace, above all in its serenity, it seems to gather all the ministering beauties of the scene into one triumphant unity.

What Mont Blanc does for this well-known shelf-walk, the Grivola does for a much less frequented walk high up on the slopes above the Cogne valley. The Dent Blanche is the feature in the view from the Alpe Créta above Evolena on the west side of the Val d'Hérens, and there is a grand walk from the Weritz alp to the Hocken alp in the Lötschental with the Bietschhorn inviting your homage all the time.

Other shelves famous for the satisfaction they give, though they lack the influence of a dominating peak, are the hog's back that runs from the Eggishorn Hotel to the Riederalp between the Rhone Valley and the Great Aletsch Glacier, the shelf above the Val d'Anniviers on which are St. Luc and Chandolin and that above the Val Fassa which ends in the Campedie, one of the most famous view-points in the Dolomites. Shorter shelves or platforms abound in the Alps and some of the most popular resorts are built upon them; Murren, the Riffelalp and Saas Fee are examples.

From a high shelf or platform you not only see the peaks from the best point of view, you have a chance of obtaining cloud effects in far greater variety than from a valley, where you can only see them from underneath. Till you have seen clouds floating around you and below you, with the sun playing all sorts of games with them, alternately turning the searchlight on them and making them vanish, they are distant strangers to you. And the spectator has always the satisfaction that the particular performance he is watching is unique. The lights upon the peaks may change in infinite variety, their forms remain the same; clouds are the expression of a mood and time that is never identical with any we have seen before or shall ever see again.

And now we come to those for whom mountain pictures and flowers and animals and birds afford pleasures incidental to a major quest. I mean those who climb the Alps because they find satisfaction in doing so, whether they reach their summits by mere walking or by the methods implied rather than described by the expression "hanging on by their eyelids"— an expression chosen, I suppose, because the eyelid, even of the most hardened winker, is peculiarly ill-adapted to prevent a fall. Mr. Geoffrey Young once obtained a really vital hold with his teeth on a repulsively protruding ledge of the Taschhorn, and many climbers must have found the teeth a useful substitute for the hands in the manipulation of the rope, but no one, as far as I know, even in the climbs recorded in the studios of the cinema, has reached the actual eyelid standard.

If you want to test your nerve and skill and live dangerously almost all the time, you will find what you require most easily in the Eastern Alps. There, a system of grading climbs by numbers from one to six, with subdivisions of lower and upper, has been adopted. For some time no climb in the Western Alps was considered by the Easterners to be difficult enough to rank as grade 6, though the south-west ridge of the Aiguille Noire de Peuteret, above Courmayeur, which led two Bavarians to the top thirty hours after leaving the hut, was by most climbers admitted to the lower sixth. Now, the north face of the Eiger and the *most direct* ascent of the north face of the Grandes Jorasses are generally admitted into the highest class. Very difficult climbing with artificial aids on precipices that not only look, but are unclimable by ordinary means has been found a

25 The Alpine Horn. In the background is the Morteratsch Glacier

26 Tyrolean Cornstooks
near Gölling-Abtenau

27 Use of *Mauerhaken* and *Karabiner* on the Wilder Kaiser

valuable agent in gaining adherence to the creed of dominance which is so assiduously taught to the youths of Germany and Italy. To many of them the word *sport*, which for want of a more national word has been adopted into both their languages, is meaningless apart from competition and a standard of measurement. If you are lucky, as well as brave and tough, you may rival some of the wonderful performances that have been accomplished by the Munich School of climbers and their Italian imitators and even survive to enjoy the satisfaction. There is no lack of climbing literature in which you may study the records of these performances.

Many climbers, especially in their early years, like the atmosphere of competition and technical achievement, and both these are to be found in their highest development within easy reach of Munich and Innsbruck, in the Kaisergebirge. If there is no professional guide there available and willing to take a visitor up a grade 6 climb, there will almost certainly be a student who will act as guide and will walk about on holdless slabs with perfect assurance. The Kaisergebirge is a perky offshoot of the Alps rather than a part of them, but it is difficult not to mention a place where there is such a concentration of the methods and ideas which have contributed so largely to the recent feats and tragedies of modern mountaineering. There the visitor will quickly become familiar with the hammer, the *Mauerhaken* (iron spikes with ring attached) and the *Karabiner* (rings that open and shut with a spring through which the rope is threaded) which are a necessary part of a modern rock-climber's equipment.

This is the sort of exercise that will earn you your night's rest, and if your nerves are good enough, you may enjoy it as well as earn it: "I hung on to the *Mauerhaken* by one hand, raised a foot to the level of my head, and with some difficulty inserted it in the sling, and then with complete ease, if not with dignity, surmounted the overhang." (N.B. This is written by a lady.) It is fair to the reader to add this warning (also written by a lady). "Anyone who values his life, however, will avoid the Kaisergebirge in July and August, and on any week-end or holiday throughout the year. At these times there are more climbers per square inch in the Kaisergebirge than in any region I know, and the stones that come down . . .!"

For those who are not attracted by competition and extremely difficult rock, who want variety of snow and ice and who prefer the majesty of repose and height in a mountain to eccentricity of form, the Western and Central Alps have most to offer.

6

There has been less systematisation than in the Eastern Alps. Ice and snow produce such varying conditions that grading is more difficult than on a rock peak; and though climbers' guides have been written for every district of the Alps, the directions become generally less detailed the further west one goes, and so away from guides of German origin, which are sometimes relentless in the strictness with which they lay down the path men are to follow. In parts of the Western Alps little more information is given than the ridge or face by which a peak may be climbed and the time taken by a fairly expert party. That is enough to give a good idea of the standard of difficulty. You will find your way by looking at the mountain, not by looking at the book, and you will find the mountain has all sorts of little surprises in store for you. In fact, you will have almost all the satisfactions of a new ascent except that of having it recorded in print.

As a field for exploration the Alps above the snow-line are a comparatively recent acquisition to the world. It is just over one hundred and fifty years since Saussure performed the opening ceremony, when he and his valet, with eighteen guides climbed to the summit of Mont Blanc. He climbed it, despite all the difficulties and the perils, real and imagined, and in defiance of the habits and prejudices of the wealthy, influential class to which he belonged, because he was an ardent scientist, and because he was also a mystic. Others followed in his steps, generally from a desire to see whether they too could perform this adventurous and arduous feat, but always carrying up thermometers or barometers or both to give the respectability of scientific research to the expedition. Very few attempted to scale any other great alpine peak. The Meyer family did some remarkable exploration in 1811 and 1812, including the ascents of the Jungfrau and Finsteraarhorn, and by the middle of the last century the satisfactions of the climber as well as those of the scientist and the explorer have appeared in the writings of Professor James Forbes, Gottlieb Studer and John Ball. The ascent of the Wetterhorn by Alfred Wills in 1854 is usually regarded as the beginning of mountaineering as an end in itself, as a sport.

In the ten years that followed, almost every peak over 12,000 feet that was then considered a separate peak was climbed. The Matterhorn, any attempt to ascend which the famous guide Christian Almer regarded as a waste of time, was ascended in 1865. The Meije, in Dauphiné, held out till 1877. Points on the ridges of the great peaks were elevated to the ranks of separate summits, the most notable being the Aiguilles on the ridges of Mont Blanc. These, and ascents by new ridges and new faces, provided the glamour of new ascents for the generations who found the field of exploration limited by the successes of their predecessors, and the supply is not yet exhausted. But the visitor to the Alps who wants to make his contribution to the yearly list of new ascents must be prepared to face extreme difficulty or extreme obscurity. Most of his exploration must be carried out in Alpine literature, not in the Alps themselves; and when you have found in it your unclimbed ridge or face or facet the exploration will be over, apart from that necessary for revealing the spot where you can place a finger or a toe, or hammer in a spike.

Climbing literature is full of the glamour of first ascents; it is the stuff that editors of mountaineering journals pray for. And so this type of literature is apt to give you an exaggerated impression of the value of mere novelty. The wise man will not let this first-ascent obsession lay its hold upon him; he will climb what takes his fancy, and in the process he will discover the satisfactions which the Alps have been holding for *him*; it is the greatest discovery he can make, and one of which no one can deprive him. And unless he is with experienced companions, he will do well, at any rate in his first year or two of climbing to take a guide for any serious expedition. Guides are outwardly smarter, younger, more obviously a part of standardised civilisation than they used to be, but as good or better climbers and with a high standard of service. If you employ a local man for a well-known peak he is likely to be thoroughly familiar with the route, to be a pleasant companion and to get you safely up and down in any ordinary conditions of weather. If you are taking men to lead you on climbs away from home ground, you will need greater care in selecting them. Intelligence, initiative, social gifts, and ability to speak the language of the district visited and pick up its local knowledge—all these have importance beside that of their knowledge of mountain craft. The opinion of those who have climbed with them is the most reliable source of information about guides.

The longer I have climbed and the more I have learned of mountains and of climbers, the more convinced I have become that the satisfactions which are won by competition with other climbers are as Dead Sea fruits compared to those which are freely offered to any able-bodied man, who regards a climb as a matter entirely between the mountain and himself or his party. The competitive element in modern life is one of the very things men go to the Alps to forget!

You may see a great deal of the Alps without ever leaving a path, but you will miss much if you never visit the ridges of the great peaks and the passes between them. There is, for every man who wishes to know the Alps intimately, as they can only be known by visiting their innermost recesses, a great field of adventure and discovery above the snow-line. The few suggestions that follow are addressed to those who would like to enter that field of adventure but are content to have their results reduced to insignificance when they are measured by modern climbing standards. The risks to life are small and now well known, but they exist and will always exist. It is a duty on all but the perfectly selfish to climb as safely as they can. For the climber himself death may be the most painless possible; often the mere shock of falling instantly paralyses many of the faculties of sensation. But an accident brings untold distress to others.

Be specially careful if you go alone. Solitary climbing has often been condemned; yet there is no way comparable to it for getting to know mountains and how to find your way upon them and for turning the light of the imagination on what they have to show us. Only be quite sure that you are not setting out to perform a difficult feat; the special satisfactions of the solitary climber are not dependent on difficulty. An easy peak climbed alone tells you more of mountains than far more difficult peaks climbed with guides who relieve you of any responsibility except that of following in their steps.

Mountaineering equipment used to be difficult to get in England at a reasonable price, if at all. Now it is obtainable within a very short distance of the Marble Arch. Before the War the only really good maps of the Alps were those of the Swiss portions on a scale of 1:50,000 and they are still the best. The contours are drawn with surprising accuracy at 30-metre intervals, blue on snow and ice, brown on pasture and black on rock or shale. There are now maps of all the Alps on the same or a larger scale; contours every 10 metres are rather too near together for clearness or accuracy.

Special maps of certain districts have been issued by foreign alpine clubs but the issues of the new maps mentioned above now supply all the information they gave and are more easily obtainable.

The reader has only to choose his district and set out, with easy-fitting boots, nailed according to the selection he may make from many styles, with an ice-axe of walking-stick length, and with garments that are numerous and light rather than few and heavy; and having endowed him with prudence, curiosity

28 *Facilis Descensus*

29 The Bondasca Spires above the Chalets of Soglio

and imagination, we may leave him to pursue his way without any more general advice.

He is one of an immense multitude "from every nation under heaven" which invades the Alps in the holiday months of summer, and repeats the invasion on a smaller scale and with more restricted objectives in the Christmas holidays. During these invasions the natives might well appear to exist for no other purpose than to minister to the needs and entertainment of the invaders and to see that they spend their money before they go away.

They have a history and a life of their own, and a very complicated history it is, politically if not socially. Only two men, Augustus and Charlemagne have ever held sway over the whole of the Alps, though Napoleon only just missed doing it. French, German and Italian are spoken and in no case (tapping wood) are all who speak the same language subjects of one political power. The Alps make nonsense of some modern racial theories. In Switzerland alone all three languages are spoken, beside two old survivals of Latin, Romonsch and Ladin, spoken in parts of the Grisons. A plebiscite among the Swiss inhabitants of the Alps would very clearly reveal that they do not regard themselves as "unredeemed" members of the larger, more powerful neighbours who speak their language. It is a remarkable thing, full of suggestion and hope for the rest of Europe that the Swiss can find in the beauty of their land and the freedom of their institutions a bond of unity that is far stronger than the disruptive influences of a different language and a different religion.

In the Western Alps the main watershed is roughly the frontier between France and Italy, and visitors are made unpleasantly aware of it at present. French is still understood in most of the valleys on the east as well as on the west of the chain, but sometimes, especially in centrally controlled places like the village post office those in official positions may refuse to use it. All this part of the Alps belonged to the old kingdom of Burgundy. When it broke up, the region of the Western Alps passed into the hands of the House of Savoy, the Dauphins of the Viennois and the Counts of Provence. The districts held by the two latter passed bit by bit into the keeping of France or the House of Savoy. The capital of this House was transferred from Chambéry to Turin in 1559. The last big change took place in 1860 when Nice and what is now Savoy were handed over to France in return for her neutrality in the struggle from which Victor Emmanuel emerged as king of Italy.

The southern slopes of Mont Blanc have not changed as regards ownership since the eleventh century, but the northern slopes with the Chamonix district suffered political changes to which most of the inhabitants were probably quite indifferent. This bit of the Alps came to Dauphiné as a marriage gift in 1268, became French in 1349, was given in exchange for other lands to Savoy in 1355, was won by Napoleon in 1792, lost again to Savoy in 1814 and given to France in 1860. It was in 1786 that a peasant of Chamonix, Jacques Balmat, accompanied by the village doctor, François Paccard, won the reward offered by Saussure for ascending Mont Blanc. The reader must judge for himself whether it is Italy or France that has the best claim to these pioneers and the contribution they bring to national pride!

From the Great St. Bernard Pass to the Monte Moro pass at the head of the Saas valley, the Pennine Alps form the frontier, and for the last few years visitors have been very much aware of it, for, except for the Théodule Pass below the Matterhorn, it has been a closed frontier. A little east of the Moro Pass the frontier runs south of the watershed and it is a strange thing to be in a country where almost everything except political allegiance and political sympathy is Italian. The Swiss conquered these southern valleys, easy of access from the north, centuries before a United Italy came into being and they have stuck to them. When you have spent some time among the folk who live there, you will hope that nothing may destroy their peace and contentment or their freedom.

Two small valleys, those of Livigno and Lei on the north side of the frontier chain, are Italian where one would expect them to be Swiss, and a very large portion of the Austrian Tyrol became Italian after the Great War, some of it containing purely German-speaking people. The names in this new Italian country are unfamiliar after their re-christening. An oldish climber might wonder what had become of the famous Drei Zinnen if he did not know they had become the Tre Cime di Lavaredo. He will be welcomed there and in any part of the Alps as of old.

One of the best things about the Alps is their power to make men forget their agitations over the political future or the political past. The further men go up into their recesses, the less they find to remind them of such things. All over the Alps the life and occupations are similar. The tourist traffic may be affected very much by a rise or fall in the exchange of a country. In 1938 the French alpine hotels were full to overflowing, while in

what was Austria a whisper of "one tourist" was said to be sometimes added to the exultant cry of "One country, one Fuehrer."
The pastoral life goes on as it has gone on for countless ages.

Pastures are usually owned by the inhabitants of the neighbouring village; occasionally they are let or sold to more distant users. On a big alp there will be at least three sets of huts,
one on each of the three zones into which the alp is divided, a
lower, a middle and a higher. There are very few villages above
6,000 feet which are inhabited all the year round. The highest
is, probably, Juf near Cresta Avers, in a high valley that branches
off from the Splugen route at Andeer; it is only just under
7,000 feet. Such a village is in the lower zone of alpine pasture.
In most valleys there is a joyful exodus of cattle and men when
the sun of summer has cleared the snow sufficiently from the
lower zone for the beasts to be taken up to it to feed. When this
has been eaten down, they move up to the middle zone and in
August they will be on the highest zone. The huts on this zone
will be as high as 8,000 feet.

If you are near these huts about milking time, you may
see a couple of men with a sort of one-legged stool strapped
on, the leg projecting where the ancestral monkey kept his
tail, moving from cow to cow and milking them into a great
frothing pail. The milk is taken straight to one of the hut
where the cheese-maker (the *Senn*) presides. It is poured into a
huge copper cauldron holding perhaps 300 litres and swung
over a fire. Rennet is added and the curd is put into presses to
make it into cheese. The cheeses are taken down to the valley
or stored in a hut which may be recognized by the stone legs
on which it stands. The herd looked after may be large and
belong to many different owners, who receive a portion of the
profits proportional to the milk yield. The vessels are kept
quite clean, but the appearance of the ground and even of the
men sometimes suggests that all the cowdung does not find
its way on to the manure heap outside the sheds.

The sheds themselves are conveniently cleaned by diverting
a small stream through them, and fastidious tourists must be
careful to see that they are not drinking water out of a channel
into which this cleansing water has previously passed.

Alpine huts have become so numerous and offer such convenient quarters that the herdsmen's huts are now rarely used
by tourists for sleeping. There are still a few places, for example
the Chavanis pastures above Cogne, where a high hay chalet
may provide a warm and fragrant alternative to a sleeping
bag or blanket on a cold night.

Alpine folk in any part of the Alps may be expected to be hospitable, as men generally are when their struggle is with nature and not with other men. And national prejudices fall away easily from those who share a shelter on a bleak hillside at 7,000 or 8,000 feet. If it were not for an occasional newspaper that comes up from the valley the things that set the politicians quarrelling would be forgotten altogether.

Some of these herdsmen and some guides too seem to live mainly on air. I remember a big strong fellow with slightly bowed legs, who came on a long winter expedition up the Mettenberg from Grindelwald whose only nourishment from beginning to end was a little dry bread and cheese and an occasional nip of gentian, the liquor made from the tall yellow flower of that name. John Addington Symonds has a story of a hearty man who had so little to form flesh and blood when at school that when he cut his finger to the bone it did not bleed!

For the Alpine peasant the cow is not sacred, but is treated with an unceasing attention not always accorded to sacred things. In addition to providing excellent food and a surplus which may be sold to buy other necessary things, it makes no small contribution to the crops of various kinds that are raised on any patches of ground that are not too steep or stony to bear them; and she supplies natural central heating to the ground floor she shares with the family.

Sheep are less frequently in evidence, but on occasions the walker may find himself an embarrassing centre of attraction for them. Sir Martin Conway was nearly carried over a precipice by the pressure of a large herd near the Wildstrubel, having somehow conveyed to them the idea that he was bringing them salt. I have myself been lifted off my feet—chaired in fact—in the dark hours of early morning on a moving mass of woolly backs near the huts on the Palü alp not far from the Bernina Hospice. On the pastures above the end of the Aletsch Glacier a huge ram with a magnificent silky fleece got a lick at my friend's rucksack and was at our heels for hours hoping to get another.

The goat is the poor man's or the poor woman's cow. It has often been credited with providing the darkish meat that is called beef and mutton on alternate days at Alpine hotels. Once, at Molveno, in the spring, I ate what was unashamedly called kid, and I found it so good that I wondered how Isaac had failed to recognize its superiority to venison. Perhaps he did, and was wise enough not to say so!

It is a healthy life these peasants lead; in the summer on the

30 Haymaking in the Allgäuer Alps

31 Juf, above Cresta Avers, the highest
Alpine village inhabited all the year
round

32 Cheese-making

33 Alpine Domestic Still-life

INTRODUCTION   33

high pastures, in the winter cutting wood, bringing it down on sledges, sawing it up and storing it, and doing all sorts of repairs and alterations to the home, while the cattle need as much attention then as in summer. But its limitations must come home to them when they see the tourist tide rise up through the valleys twice a year, bringing evidences of the wealth to be made in cities and of all the things that wealth can buy. Inevitably it must create in many of the young a longing to see these cities and try their fortune in them. And it is more than the desire to make money that induces thousands of them to go away and take very humble, hard places as under-porters, waiters or domestic servants in other countries. Nearly all of them come back, after a varying period of years, to the hill country where they were born. They cannot bear the thought of final separation from it.

From such people one would not expect great works of art; no one goes to the Alps to see pictures and buildings. Art is best where there are men who have seen beauty and feel the need of re-creating it to enrich their lives; the most imaginative work has often come from men compelled to pass most of their days in shabby, slummy places where ugly things obtrude themselves on every side. The less obtrusive man's work is the better, in places where nature offers a feast of beauty every day, where beauty is taken for granted as the accompaniment of life. A noble building in flat country supplies a need that anyone can feel who sees it. The spires of our cathedrals and churches can gather our thoughts and lift them above the earth; for the Alpine folk, the peaks supply in more generous measure than man can ever do the beauty and dignity of form which it is the pride of architecture to achieve.

Simplicity, utility and resistance to the elements are what we find in buildings in the Alps. Yet there, as in other places, the soul of the people is shown whenever it has attempted to express itself in art that is not mere imitation. Among the few really interesting examples of native art, the most characteristic are the inscriptions carved on the beams of chalets and huts, outside and inside. The following are typical; they are taken from a paper by Mr. Walter Larden on inscriptions in the Lötschental. The first is on the balcony of a house built at Ried in 1728.

IN. IAR. DA. MAN. ZALT. 170ᵴ. DVO. IST. VNS. GOT. BEI. GESTANDEN. DVO. IST. DIE. BACHELĀ. ZV. BEDEN. SITEN. DEM. HAVS. AB. GANGEN. (In the year when one counted 1703, then did God stand by us. Then did the avalanche in the Bach gorge go past the house on either side.)

This is from a herdsman's hut on the Telli-alp.

Im Jahr 1814. Gott Gesegne Menschen und Fich In diser Hitten vor Allem Besem Ungewiter. (In the year 1814, May God bless men and cattle in this hut against all dangerous storms.)

And this last is from a house at Wyler rebuilt after a fire in 1905.

In der Nähe Maria baue ich Peter Bellwald zum zweiten mal.
     Des Glaubens Baum bringt Frucht der Tugend
     Drum pflanze ihn in zarter Jugend.
Gewiss ist der Tod; ungewiss der Tag u. die Stund, Zeit und Ort.
(Near (the chapel of) Maria, I, Peter Bellwald, rebuild my house. The tree of faith bears virtue as its fruit; therefore plant it in tender youth. Certain is Death; uncertain the day, the hour, the time and place.)

If we were to put that sort of decoration on our houses in England we should be classed with the men who walk about with texts round their hats. In high mountains man is less self-conscious and more conscious of the forces round him which are outside human control. Sometimes, as in Tibet, the action of these forces is ascribed to devils; in the Alps, the greater part of the mountain people have faith in an all-seeing, controlling power, to whom acts of hospitality, honesty and loyalty are acceptable gifts. That is why travellers in so many regions of the Alps may pursue their way without fear of giving or suffering offence and with the certainty that help will be given spontaneously and generously should they find themselves in need of it.

In recent years notices have appeared in some of the approaches to the frontier warning people that they may be shot if they venture along certain paths; and incidents have happened which show that the warning is not an idle one. Well! We were told long ago that offences must come; happily, when an offence comes, like a pestilence, it also goes; men always learn in time that life is better without it! In a few years the present acute fever of nationalism will have worn itself out, and these frontier prohibitions will be a thing of the past. Even the smuggler may have disappeared. Common sense has begun to remove the high duties which are the foundation of his trade. His romantic figure stealing with his sack of coffee or tobacco across the pass—generally at night because he fears the jaws of the crevasses less than the rifles of the *douaniers*—may soon cease to have any existence in fact. He will continue to live a glorified life in the wonderful tales that have been told about him in the literature of the Alps, from Töpffer to Charles Gos.

There is only one attractive type of guard-house or custom-house in the Alps, and that is one in ruins. It is pleasant to think that the young generation growing up may be able to stroll across every Alpine frontier freely, from whatever side they come, and enjoy the atmosphere of freedom that is proper to any Alpine pasture. There are few sights more refreshing to the senses and the soul than that of men engaged in the simplest and oldest of all productive work, in a free land under a free sky, learning the things that belong to the peace that emanates from all great mountains, a peace that relies on something better than costly frontier defences to secure it.

II

THE SOUTH-WESTERN ALPS

ON one of the low hills that rise just outside Turin on its east side is the church of the Superga. If you climb to the top of the dome on a clear day, you will realise what an immense mountain barrier runs round the edge of the North Italian plain. South, west and north is a chain of peaks that never lose their snow, and that means that they must be more than 10,000 feet in height.

Four peaks have pre-eminence over all their immediate neighbours; the Argentera almost due south of you, Monte Viso south-west by west, the Levanna, north-west, and the Gran Paradiso north-west by north. The most famous of all these south-western Alps, the Ecrins and the Meije in Dauphiné, stand so far behind the central portion of the chain that they do not show over it. These peaks mark the districts which are of special interest in the portion of the Alps dealt with in this chapter.

The Argentera is the highest point of what I may call the seaward Alps, those from which the Mediterranean is visible. Some of the first men to reach the high summits further north, even as far as Mont Blanc, thought they saw the sea, but the unimaginative laws of mathematics are against them. It is hard to decide where these seaward Alps begin. If perpetual snow is our test, then we must not go east of the Colle di Tenda, for there is no glacier of any sort in the continuation of the Alps on that side of it. For me this line of division cuts off from the Alps a district which I have only refrained from re-visiting for fear a second visit might impair the perfect memories of the first. That visit was made in April, when peaks of 7,000 feet are well above the snow line, as far as a snow-line can be said to exist when slopes at 6,000 feet may be bare in certain aspects and others under deep snow at 3,000, and slopes of every sort above 2,000 may carry a foot of new snow a couple of days later! If you visit any Alps in April without ski, these are the Alps to choose. The tourist tide is at low water mark; day after day, as soon as you leave the zone of winter habitation you have the mountains for an undisturbed possession. Nothing sharpens the appreciation more than contrast. And spring time in the Alps that form the protecting wall behind the Riviera will give it you in generous measure. First of all, in the snow itself. On the upper slopes of the Mont Clapier I have found it crisp and firm, like a springy floor pushing me up the mountain. Two or three days previously I had been ploughing through it up to my thighs on the Marguareis, the highest of the Ligurian Alps which continue the chain east of Tenda. I had only escaped from its clutches by a hazardous descent into the Val Pesio as night fell. How much the value of security and ease can be enhanced by hours of battle! When I passed the Certosa di Pesio, with its avenues of great trees and half mile of cloisters, then in perfect peace and solitude under the moon, I thought it must be the loveliest place in all the Alps in which to stay and dream. In summer it is now an excellent hydropathic establishment and not a place of solitude. The Besimauda can be ascended either from here or from Limone on the Nice-Turin railway; the ascent is easy from either side and the view of the Alps is finer than from any other point of such a modest height; it is just under 8,000 feet.

Then, within an hour or two you may pass from winter into summer in this part of the world in spring. I did so on my first short expedition from Ormea where the railway up the Val Tanara ends. On the slopes facing north all was in the grip of winter a short way above the town. Bare trees rose forlornly out of the snow; on the rock faces great icicles hung down, the drops even at mid-day freezing at their tips as they hesitated in the wind. Then, as I crossed the ridge and looked on the sea, I came into a different world. Quite a short way down these southern slopes the streams were escaping from their prison under the snow; primroses and violets appeared wherever the earth was bare and I came upon great patches where the crocuses were so thick I could not walk without trampling on them. Round the first houses men were getting to work with mattocks in the fields and the blossom was coming out on the fruit trees. Blossom is one of the best gifts of spring anywhere, but seen here against a glistening background of snowy hillside, there was a suggestion of bridal adornment that seemed to make the day a special one in the earth's life and in mine. The young grass had begun to grow and in the hot sun it was warm to the hand, inviting me, in a way it was impossible to refuse to lie down and listen to the stir of all kinds of happy, newly-wakened things.

And you will not easily find a greater contrast in the people you may meet. I have never met simpler, kindlier folk than those

7

with whom I lodged at Viozène, before ascending the Marguareis; their faces had some of the qualities of the big things
among which they lived; they were good to look at. I will
attach no epithets to the people I met two days later in the
afternoon train on their way to Monte Carlo; they offered the
strongest possible contrast to my mountain hosts. The experience I have quoted was typical of what I found in this district.

One thing you must not fail to do, if you can still go up a
hill without a car or a *téléférique*; that is, to climb up to some
point which gives a view northward to the distant Alps as well
as over the sea. If your ambition rises to the Argentera, you
must approach it from Italy. It is a rock climb, not very difficult, either from the Genova hut, four hours above Entraque,
or from the Baths of Valdieri which is a much lower starting
point. The upper part of the route lies on the east face and it is
not safe till the snow has come away from the slopes above;
that will not be till near the end of June at the earliest in a
normal year. The Roccia dell'Abisso, despite its name, is easily
reached from Vievola on the road and railway just south of
Tenda. It commands a superb view of the Alps and sea. Unfortunately it also commands a view of the forts on the Italian
side and access to it has been, before and since the War, forbidden. I nearly got stuck for good in a seemingly endless
valley of deep snow, endeavouring to escape the observation of
the military authorities some years ago, and the nationality
nuisance is worse than it was then.

The best peaks in the district to aim for at any season of the
year are the Mont Clapier and the Cima dei Gelas. In order
that King Victor Emmanuel might continue to enjoy his old
hunting grounds, the frontier was drawn some miles south of
these peaks on the main watershed. There are no forts near and
in spring certainly you may cross the frontier without knowing you have done so in either of the valleys of approach. In
the Val Gordolasca you cross it some time before reaching the
Rifguio Nizza at about 7,000 feet. From here you can climb
the Mont Clapier, which offers no difficulty to an active man,
or the Mont Gelas, which is a most attractive little peak, most
easily reached from a broad terrace that runs across its east
face above the Lago Lungo, not far from the hut. With good
snow you can climb both peaks and be back in the hut in time
to let a hot sun dry the seat of your trousers if you have wet
them by glissading.

The view from either peak includes the best features of
views from other points on the main watershed; the near view

34   The mid-August Pilgrimage at Bessans

35   An Alpine Town: Saint Martin de Vésubie

from the Gelas is better, the view northwards slightly freer from the Mont Clapier. Of all summit views this is the one that has impressed me most. On one side the sea and the Riviera coast; beyond it the Carrara mountains and the peaks of Corsica. On the other side, running north, then in the far distance turning east, the Alps. Monte Viso catches the eye at once, standing head and shoulders above anything near it; the Matterhorn is not hard to pick out in the Pennine Alps; further east they fade away into dim blue outlines which you may or may not be right in calling Disgrazia and Adamello. Between you and them is an immense plain covered by a faint mist through which are seen suggestions of rivers, spires of churches and the smoke from busy towns.

There is an excellent approach to the Gelas from the Madonna delle Finestre, less than three hours' walk from St. Martin de Vésubie and 6,000 feet up. There is a hotel open in summer and a hut open at all times. It is a delightful place for a climber or a walker or a botanist. There, as in all parts of this district, the flowers are good, whether they are rare plants that are hardly found at all elsewhere or those that rejoice us by their abundance. I say, are good, but I speak of some years ago before the flower-robbers had multiplied. *Saxifraga florulenta, saxifraga lantoscana, Silene cordifolia* and others may still reward the searcher after botanical trophies *lantoscana* being Latin for "found near Lantosque," the village in the valley below the junction of the Vésubie and Gordalasca glens.

All the roads that lead up into the seaward Alps, to the villages of St. Martin de Vésubie, St. Sauveur and Beuil pass through limestone gorges, and they are not roads for learner drivers. The most thrilling is that leading to Beuil, through the gorges of the Cian. In places this road is just a groove cut in the vertical precipice above the torrent, a tunnel with one side open through which there is an assured exit from the world into the abyss below. I have actually passed a car on a bad stretch; if I had not been going down and had the inside I should have got out without any hesitation. We nestled up against the wall of the precipice while the other car crept past. Its driver made his companion get out so that one at least should survive. There was less than three inches between the outer wheels and the edge; the edge, not the curb, for the roadway just ended in a sharp clean line of rock above a clear drop; I cannot give a figure for the time a car would have taken to reach the stream, if it had gone over; there was nothing it could have touched and there could not possibly have been

36 (opposite)
The Meige from La Grave

anything worth retrieving at the bottom. So far, they told me at Beuil, there had been no accident, which shows that Nature's warnings are more effective than those of road authorities.

Beuil is quite a fashionable winter sports place. The village itself may be almost clear of snow in April, but the road continues westward towards Guillaume, and a mile or two along it I saw a scene on the snow-covered pastures near it which reminded me of the shore at Llandudno or Southport, both in its numbers and in the sounds that came from it, for high inarticulate cries are much the same, whether they come from French or British lips.

Roads are being made to connect the upper parts of these seaward valleys. That from St. Martin de Vésubie over the Col St. Martin to St. Delmas and thence past a new fort in an amazing position at Rimplas to St. Sauveur is open now. It passes through a short tunnel on the Col St. Martin, which was being made when I went through it. My entrance into the tunnel coincided with the short interval between the signal for blasting and the blast itself. I waited behind a sandbag barrier till the bangs came. There were seven bangs and should have been eight; all the lights went out and portions of the roof fell. The man crouching near me said: *"il y a un qui dort"*; in consequence my walk through the next stretch of tunnel was unenjoyable. It is a varied and beautiful road and the colours on the rocks near St. Sauveur are extraordinary.

There is no road pass over the Alps between the Col de Tenda and the Col de Larche, which was better known till lately as the Col de l'Argentière, one of the five passes claimed as Hannibal's pass. The "Route des Alpes" keeps to the left at the entrance to every one of the three valleys that lead up to St. Martin de Vésubie, St. Sauveur and Beuil. In winter it adopts a very sub-alpine route by Digne and Sisteron and the Col de Lus-la-Croix-Haute to Grenoble. As the snow melts in May and June more alpine routes can be taken and at some time in June both the Col d'Allos (7,380 feet) and the Col de la Cayolle (7,720 feet) should be clear and offer alternative ways of driving to Barcelonnette. Allos in the Verdon valley at about 4,600 feet is a good centre, almost unknown to English travellers; among its attractions are flowers of many species, a lake at over 7,000 feet with boats upon it and many fish in it, *maisons forestières* in which visitors can get permission to spend the night above 6,000 feet and a number of small peaks; the highest is the Mont Pelat which just passes the 10,000 feet mark and is easy of access from the lake. It offers a steep rock climb from the Cayolle glen, through which runs the road descending from the Col de la Cayolle. This road joins that from the Col d'Allos at Barcelonnette in the pleasant, fertile valley of the Ubaye. A few miles up this valley the road is joined by that from the Col de Larche coming in from the east. That Col is the northern limit of this first section of the South-western Alps, and it has already taken more than the share the map would give it in this chapter. Not more than it deserves. Its features are not easily forgotten: wonderful limestone gorges whose walls carry an untouchable wealth of beauty, flowers in profusion, including many rare kinds, picturesque villages and isolated chapels perched on rocky heights, and peaks which may be of modest height and small reputation compared with the giants of the Alps but which give the man who reaches their summits on a good day hours that are some of the most cherished in all his alpine memories.

North of the Col de Larche we come to the Cottian Alps. The name *Alpis Cottia* was given by the Romans to the pass of the Mont Genèvre, one of the very few passes across the Alps which they knew by name. This pass or the Mont Cenis pass a little north of it is the northern limit of these Cottian Alps. One splendid mountain dominates the whole district, Monte Viso; its supremacy is unmistakable, whether you see it from one of the peaks that surround it on three sides or from the plains round Turin; every valley of special interest in this region leads towards it. There are five of them that deserve mention. One is the valley of the Ubaye, by which we have just left the Maritime Alps; it leads up from the south-west and is entirely French. It has an Italian opposite in which French is still spoken, the Val Pellice, which comes in from the north. Neither of these valleys goes right up to the Viso, but only up to the inner ring of peaks which usher you into his presence, and let you see his full magnificence.

Of the remaining three valleys one is the French valley of the Guil that runs in a great curve from Guillestre to the north-west foot of the Viso; the two on the Italian side are the upper Po valley which offers the only good approach for those who wish to climb the mountain, and the Val Varaita which divides at the village of Casteldelfino into wild glens, one of which, the Val Vallante, runs up from the south under the precipices of the Viso to the frontier pass of the Col Vallante between the Viso on the east and the Pointe Joanne or Cima di Losetta on the west. When the frontier is open you can descend from it into the upper Guil valley.

The Ubaye valley above St. Paul, where the buses of the Route des Alpes turn left to climb up to the Col de Vars, was till quite recently beyond the reach of motorists. Only five years ago it was written: "*L'automobiliste ne saurait s'aventurer dans cette austère region.*" Now, petrol will take you to Maljasset in the hollow of Maurin at the head of the valley, at over 6,000 feet. It is surprising that so little has been done in the past to make Maljasset a more attractive centre. The best that Professor Coolidge could say of it in 1879 was "the accommodation was rather rough, but the food, as far as it went, tolerable," and the French quotation above shows that improvement, if any, was small. Where motorists venture, climbers may go without fear, provided the hotel has a means of access other than the road. Maljasset is surrounded by peaks of about 11,000 feet. The Brec de Chambeyron is a grand sight as one looks back across the valley driving up to the Col de Vars. Both it and the Aiguille de Chambeyron can be climbed from the high pass between them. The Aiguille has the advantage of being entirely in France, so that there is no excuse for a fascist soldier to have a pot at you; it is also more difficult than the Brec, which some will find an advantage, others will not; the Alps can suit all tastes. Near the head of the valley on the right is the Grand Rubren. Its ascent is perfectly easy and the view of the Viso across a deeply cut valley is magnificent.

The lower part of the next big valley to the north, the Guil Valley consists of a series of gorges cut through the Combe de Queyras. Till the present century the only exits from the Guil valley above Château Queyras were paths that climbed on to the mountain sides at vast heights above the river. Now a remarkable road traverses the gorges, crossing and recrossing the torrent and often gouged out of the perpendicular sides of the immense cleft which it has cut. It is one of the most spectacular bits of road in the Alps and the "Route des Alpes" includes it, reaching Briançon by turning north-west over the Col d'Izouard just before passing the small, grandly placed fortress of Château Queyras. Two miles further up the Guil valley is Aiguilles, the "capital" of the valley and distinguished from the usual rather miserable, if picturesque, collection of buildings that constitute an Alpine village by a girdle of elegant villas that testify to the reality of the fortunes made in Brazil and other parts of the Americas by enterprising emigrants who have returned.

The road is motorable for several miles further. Abriès is a popular holiday resort and the highest place suitable for a long

37 Monte Viso from the North-East

38 Les Écrins

39 Les Grandes Rousses through the Brèche de la Meige

stay. The road continues up the long valley as far as the Roche Ecoulée, a sort of rocky grand stand from which to view the Viso, and it is worth coming a long way to see it. At the valley-head we may take either of two passes into Italy, or rather we shall be able to take them when smiles instead of bullets welcome the wanderer who strolls across the frontier. On the left, under the Monte Granero is the way to the Col de la Traversette, the crest of which is pierced by a tunnel made in the fifteenth century to facilitate the passage of men and beasts. After a stony descent from this pass on the Italian side we come to a wholly delightful spot, the Piano del Re, where parties can picnic and contemplate the rocky face of the Viso seamed by a broad steep band of snow that ends in overhanging cliffs of ice.

The infant Po makes its first appearance near by, bursting up among the boulders; and it is not unlikely that the small glacier hanging on the face of the Viso gives it its start in life.

A few miles down the valley is Crissolo, the best headquarters for a stay near the Viso on the Italian side. A quarter of an hour's walk from the village is the Sanctuary of San Chiaffredo; on the feast day of the saint, processions of pilgrims in picturesque costume wend their way to it, but on other days the view of the Viso, which is not seen from Crissolo itself, is the most attractive feature of the shrine. The wonderful cave called the Caverna del Rio Martino is another of the sights of Crissolo and less than half an hour's walk from it. There is a good path from Crissolo to the Rifugio Quintino Sella, a small hotel beside a lake at over 8,000 feet, under the Viso Mozzo. This is the place to sleep in if you intend to climb the Viso. The great east face of that peak rises straight up from the other side of the lake. The summit is out of sight behind, but a huge tower on the east ridge is admirably placed to convey the impression of immense height. Close at hand is the stony pass called the Col dei Viso between the Viso and the Viso Mozzo. On the other side of this pass, an easy gradual descent leads down under the high shattered ridge connecting the Viso with the Col de la Traversette to the Piano del Re.

The easiest way to climb the Viso is to go a short distance south-west to the Sagnette pass and cross the stony slopes to the base of the south face, where there is a hut belonging to the Italian Alpine Club, and then ascend the south face in zig-zags. The summit is crowned by a cross twenty feet high and a statue of the Madonna. The route up the east face, first taken by that most romantic of all Italian climbers, Guido Rey, is far more interesting and not really difficult. If a way is well chosen up the rock face above the lake, the danger of falling stones in the lower part of Rey's route will be avoided. When taking a friend up the east face I followed the written descriptions and began the climb close to a deep gully that comes down near the Col dei Viso, then crossed the face under the great tower to reach the slopes on its south side by which it can be turned and the east ridge gained above it. After this there is a climb up splendid rocks, with an occasional traverse on steep snow. But in the lower part of the climb below the tower stones fell repeatedly. We saw a few of them, but the majority passed unseen above our heads singing on a note that indicated an extremely high velocity.

The hut below the south face may be reached direct from Casteldelfino by the Forciolline glen. At Casteldelfino there is, as the name suggests, an old castle of the Dauphins (built in the fourteenth century) and it is the starting point for the Pelvo d'Elva, one of the peaks that may fairly claim the finest view of the Viso. It has few other permanent attractions. In 1879 Professor Coolidge, a mine of information on all Alpine matters wrote of its hospitality: "The food was not remarkably good, and the prices not very low. The hostess is well-meaning, but fussy and rather flighty." A hostess who could be flighty with Coolidge should have been a better draw than a star in Baedeker, but her brightness had long waned when Sir Martin Conway visited it in 1896.

Since then the motor-car has arrived—and Mussolini—bringing noise, cleanliness and commercial enterprise.

The Val Pellice is the most northerly of the valleys that radiate from the Viso. History has linked it with the Val Chisone, which runs almost parallel to the Dora Riparia, the broad valley which separates the Cottian Alps from the Graians and through which passes the main line from France to Turin. These two, the Val Pellice and the Val Chisone are the best known of the Waldensian valleys. The religious zeal of the Vaudois or Waldensians goes back to a religious revival at Lyons in the twelfth century; in the sixteenth century they voluntarily joined in with the Geneva Calvinists and suffered persecution in consequence, not gaining full liberty of worship till after a heroic resistance lasting through many generations. They won the sympathy of fellow protestants in many countries, not least in England; at Bobbio, a large village where the motor road ends, a dam was built to protect the place from inundations with a grant from Oliver Cromwell. There are no great peaks and no glaciers to be seen; it is the history of the people, the clear streams and fine woods that are the attractions of these Waldensian valleys. Easy passes lead from one to another. The Col de Sea Bianca is one of the pleasantest, and here one may—or certainly might some years ago—find a kind of arabis that was found nowhere else but in these valleys, as its name *pedemontana* suggests. Official prohibitions, but no natural obstacles, prevent pleasant expeditions over the frontier from the Val Pellice to the upper Guil Valley and Abriès. Without crossing the frontier, however, it is possible to visit either the Monte Meidassa or the Monte Granero from the pass between them and contemplate the northern facets of the Viso; this is its snowiest and for that reason perhaps its best side. Prolonged contemplation may induce a desire to climb the peak by a rather difficult and complicated way up the north-west face or by a difficult and dangerous way up the north-east.

The Val Pellice above Bobbio is one of the secluded places where the smell of petrol never offends. The Val Chisone on the other hand has for many years had a road up to its head and over the Col de Sestrières to Césanne. (Mind you call it Cesana when you are in it.) Sestrières is now a well-known winter sports place and must be one of the highest, being near the pasture plateau of the Col, which is 6,630 feet. Césanne is at the foot of the great road pass of the Mont Genèvre between Briançon and Oulx, and here we must leave the Cottians for the Dauphiné Alps.

These have innumerable good things for the climber and a great deal for the botanist. The former must always rank the district high, for it contains the Meije. The Meije held out longer against assault than any other great mountain in the Alps—I do not include obelisks, or peaks under 12,000 feet, however difficult to climb, among the great peaks of the Alps. Mountaineering will be far advanced in decadence when climbers cease to regard a traverse of the Meije as one of the very best things in the Alps. Modern climbers have higher standards of technique and go faster than the early conquerors of the Alps; and it must be remembered that many of the latter were comparatively unathletic men. Even the best of the old guides were more deliberate movers than the young professional expert of to-day. The first parties to climb the Meije were thankful to get down the same way and spent a very uncomfortable night upon it on the way down. The ridge of savage-looking teeth which connects the highest western point with the "Doigt de Dieu" or Pic Central was first traversed by the brothers Zsigmondy with Purtscheller in 1885; four hours was con-

8

sidered pretty good time for this crossing from one peak to the
other. In 1911 Mr. Young and Josef Knubel took six and a
half hours only, excluding halts, to cross the peak from the
Promontoire hut to La Grave. Perhaps there are now men
who consider this rather slow time!

The huge rock wall that forms the south face of the Meije
as it is seen at the head of the Etançons glen from near La
Bérarde is a thing to rejoice a climber's heart, but it is far less
beautiful than the thousands of feet of ice-hung precipice that
hold every eye in every car as it approaches La Grave, coming
up from Bourg d'Oisans. One longs too, at La Bérarde, for
stretches of green pasture amid the profusion of stones and ice
and precipice.

The comb-like ridge of the Ecrins is the highest in the district. Unlike the Meije, the Ecrins shuns publicity; the only
road from which you can realize what a splendid peak it is,
is the upper part of that which runs from Le Lautaret to the
Col du Galibier. The north face, which is seen from there,
rises above one of the whitest and loveliest glaciers in the Alps,
the Glacier Blanc. Near the end of this glacier, at 8,200 feet is
the Tuckett hut, easily reached from Ville Vallouise. From here
the Pic de Neige Cordier, a splendid view-point, much less
difficult of access than the Ecrins or the Meije, can be ascended
from the Col Emile Pic on the way over to the Chalet de l'Alpe.
This small hotel is in a broad green valley, delightfully secluded
yet easily reached in a couple of hours from either La Grave
or Le Lautaret. The beautiful snow peak at the head of the
green valley is the Montagne des Agneaux, which, like the Pic
de Neige Cordier puts no special difficulties in the way of those
who are wise enough to climb it and enjoy an exceptionally fine
view of things near and far away.

Other Dauphiné peaks, the Pelvoux, the Ailefroide, the Pic
d'Olan, etc.—their name is legion—will keep a climber happily
employed for many weeks, though they do not challenge the
supremacy of those twin stars Les Ecrins and La Meije.

The Dauphiné Alps have things to offer besides glacier and
precipice. Some of the pastures that surround the central chaos
of high peaks have long been celebrated for their flowers,
especially those behind La Grave and around the Col du
Lautaret. No one who has stayed at Le Lautaret will wonder
at the Romans having erected there a small temple which only
exists now in the name (Collis de altareto). Here there are many
treasures for the flower-seeker. Will it be possible to say the
same twenty years hence? The motor-car is a terrible menace

40 The Road to Beuil

41 Mont Pelvoux from the Tuckett Refuge

42　The Glacier des Agneaux

43　The Grivola from the North

to the gems that are strewn about the pastures near the Col and in those between it and the Col du Galibier. These last used to be secluded places visited only by an occasional friend familiar with their beauties; now the new road circling high upon the hillsides brings scores of car-loads every day within a few minutes' walk of these flourishing colonies of flowers. It is almost inevitable that a ribbon development of desolation will be the result, and it is a poor consolation to know that a few specimens may be preserved, like museum pieces, in the Alpine garden recently constructed near the P.L.M. hotel at Le Lautaret.

In the Dauphiné district, but even more outlying than the group of great peaks described above, are the ranges of the Grandes Rousses and Belledonne. The Grandes Rousses carry plenty of summer snow and respectable glaciers and they rise well above 11,000 feet. The Belledonne range has many attractive rock climbs on it, but the summer sun strips all the snow from it, as it fails to reach 10,000 feet rank. Both ranges are conveniently near Grenoble and Lyons, where are the homes of hundreds of French climbers; English climbers, when they go far from home, are naturally more attracted to bigger things.

North of La Grave three rocky pyramids rise in a line, high above a wilderness of stones; these are the Aiguilles d'Arves. The southern aiguille has a short, difficult bit of climbing on it which certainly justifies its name of *mauvais pas*; it gives a climber considerable satisfaction to have surmounted it. These three gaunt examples of Nature's powers of denudation are a long way from any road; I doubt if anybody has ever seen them from a car, and that is rather a distinction now for an Alpine peak.

North of the Mont Cenis pass and south of the Val d'Aosta is a collection of mountain groups known as the Graian Alps. They are much better known to English visitors than the Cottians or the Maritimes. They cannot compete with the Dauphiné Alps for the favour of men in their prime who want to test their climbing powers; for them the faces of the Ecrins, the Meije and the Ailefroide are divinely fair. The Graians will be the choice of those who prefer beauty that is less invariably severe.

There are at least four places in the Graians which possess the things that favourites among Alpine centres should possess; altitude, good quarters, green pastures, streams, flowers, and plenty of peaks to look at as well as to climb. The order of merit in which I place them is based purely on personal preference, Cogne, Val d'Isère, Cérésole, Bonneval. Some people would add a fifth, Pralognan, but it is rather shut in, and for nearly all the chief climbs you have first to go to the inn on the Col de la Vanoise, which is 3,500 feet above it.

All five can be reached by car. Bonneval and Val d'Isère, both at 6,000 feet, are now connected by a new road over the Col du Mont Iseran. The completion of this road has meant a pilgrimage from all the motorists who like their car to have been over the highest pass in the Alps; for the Col du Mont Iseran is more than thirty feet higher than the Stelvio, whose 9,055 feet previously held the record. Cogne is just over 5,000 feet; Motor-buses go up frequently from Aosta, leaving the main valley road near Aymaville. Parts of the road are a tight fit for two cars and hardly a fit at all when one is a bus; many mudguards must carry away scars from encounters with various objects moving or unremoved. Do not let that deter you from visiting it. There is no place which more persuasively calls back the visitor who wants what the Alps themselves have to offer, rather than what has been imported into them by modern life. There is no golf course, I doubt if there are tennis courts, though there are plenty of cheery, talkative Italian families staying there. The road really stops there; some who simply cannot or will not walk use their cars when they travel two miles up the valley to have tea with strawberries and cream at Lilla, but there is no through traffic.

The drive up from Aymaville is, for all but the driver, particularly attractive. You start up at once after crossing the rushing Dora Baltea which is carrying down quite a lot of the crumbled rocks of Mont Blanc, and pass through orchards and small vineyards and other evidences of sun-favoured slopes; then you bend round the hill-side northwards above Pont d'El. It is worth descending to look at this bridge, which still carries the original inscription telling you it was built in the reign of Augustus. It has been thrown across the deep gorge of the Grand' Eyvia, the torrent that drains the Cogne valley; below the footway of the bridge is a vaulted acqueduct that carried water as well as men and beasts across. After passing Pont d'El the road and valley bend eastward, so that as we near Cogne and look back, it is the Mont Blanc range that forms the sky-line of the westward view. Above, on the right, there have been glimpses of the north face of the Grivola, which is one of Nature's very best examples of modelling on the grand scale.

Aosta is a hot place on a fine summer day, and the temptation to let petrol take you up to Cogne is generally irresistible. It is a pity; for the northern slopes of the huge Mont Emilius are not sun-heated early in the day and new beauties in the view are revealed at almost every step of the way to Cogne. When you have passed the sanctuary of St. Grat and the Chamole huts, you can go either south-west over the Col du Drinc and descend to Epinel in the valley three miles from Cogne, or better still, over the Col de Chaz Sèche and so past the Arpisson chalets and Gimilian to the main valley at Cogne itself. Descending from either col the Grivola is a superb object and the photographer will be kept busy, for each small variation in the subject will make him wonder whether it is not even better than the last he took. If you want to add a summit to your walk, the Becca di Nona and the Mont Emilius are there for you to choose. But you will do well to spend a night at the hut near the Arbole lake or at the Comboe chalets, for the difference of height is nearly 10,000 feet in the case of Mont Emilius and only 1,000 feet less for its neighbour.

Cogne, when you reach it, is a village large enough and old enough to boast a bishop, with a "village green" of some hundred acres, made a good many years ago by the materials brought by torrents down the Valnontey which comes in from the south. You look up its full length from Cogne to the central portion of the ring of high peaks that enclose it, with the Col de Grand Croux in the centre looking just what a pass should be, a real depression approached by a glacier that does not let you forget its hidden depths and confronts you at the end with a wall which you prefer to be decorated in snow white rather than in ice blue and which adds a spice of excitement to the other attractions its ascent provides.

Three peaks, all on the east side of the Valnontey, are climbed far oftener than any others near Cogne, the Grivola, the Herbetet, and the Grand Paradis—pardon—I mean the Gran Paradiso. For the Grivola, it is usual to sleep at the Italian alpine club hut in the Lauson glen, above the royal camping place, crossing over the Colle della Nera in the morning on to the upper part of the Trajo Glacier and climbing up the east face. If the best way is taken there is no serious difficulty, but a look-out must be kept for loose rocks coming down when you cross from one rib to another, especially if there are parties above. Last time I was on this face I was surprised to find bits of scarlet paper on the rocks and overtook the decorators in the shape of two Germans, who, with their usual thoroughness, had been making sure of not losing their way coming down. Needless to say they were the old type of German climber, slow and sure, not the modern sort, who think nothing of being benighted for two or three nights running and hang their lives on pitons every few yards on faces unclimbable by natural means.

Since the opening of the hut in the Lauson glen the standard of cleanliness at the Pousset chalets where one used to sleep has deteriorated. You must sleep there or at the Grand Nomenon huts if you attempt the Grivola by the north ridge, and the latter are certainly best if you have doubts about the descent on to the Nomenon glacier from the col just north of the Grivoletta. The upper part of the north ridge is an exposed climb; which means that most men will be glad of all the security that good steps and sharp crampons can give them against taking what would be their last slide down the thousand feet or so of glassy wall, which their efforts have put between themselves and the apparently flat surface of the glaciers on either side.

The Herbetet is approached from the chalet de l'Herbetet; you must decide for yourself whether a night there is worth the two and a half hour's walk it saves in the morning. It is easy to miss it in the dark. For the Gran Paradiso there is no choice; an early start is essential, perhaps before dancing has stopped at the Belvedere Hotel, so that a late supper takes the place of pre-dawn *café*; everyone knows what a difference a name makes in this case. One of the features of this district is the magnificent provision of paths for the mule that conveyed a royal master to a hunting *gîte*. They are for hunting, not climbing, and do not always lead where the mountaineer wishes them to lead. When the path ends at the head of the Valnontey, there will be a chance for the guide of the party, if it is without local professional talent, to find the very best way on to the Tribulation Glacier, which, in my experience, does not justify its name. Once on this glacier, the man with a climber's guide in his pocket or an instinct for route-finding in his head will proceed to climb the Gran Paradiso or any minor summit near that takes his fancy. An ascent of the Gran Paradiso is a reason for visiting the Victor Emmanuel hut, I might almost say an excuse for such a visit, for it is a delectable place, and the way down to it is the easiest route in the Alps on a peak over 13,000 feet, except the ordinary route on the Zermatt Breithorn. This hut is perfectly situated at the upper limit of the pastures, above the Moncorvé Glacier. Here the clucking of hens and the tinkling of cow-bells remind one pleasantly of food which has never been inside a rucksack; across the glacier are four peaks, of which the two furthest to the right are irresistibly attractive, one, the Becca di Monciair from the loveliness of its form, the other, the Punta di Broglio because it makes one long to find

44 Cogne and the Valnontey

45 The *dépendance* of the Monei Chalets above Cogne
—three brethren

46 Pralognan in the
    Val d'Isère

47 Roccia Viva from
    the Tour du Grand
    St. Pierre

out if its highest point is accessible at all. The hut can be reached in about two hours from Pont at the head of the Valsavaranche or from Cérésole over a choice of easy passes in five or six hours.

There is a pasture shelf on the east side of the Valnontey from which the ridge of peaks from the Gran Paradiso to the Grivola provides a most satisfying subject for contemplation and the chalet de Monei built upon it will provide for more material wants. A climber could spend a week here without exhausting the climbs on this east side of the valley.

The main valley continues east of Cogne with valleys and hunting paths coming in from the south. Up these side valleys there will rarely be any party but your own. Signs of tourist visitors are few, and even the royal paths show how rapidly Nature obliterates man's ordering of the way in mountain country, now that the king has ceased to pay his regular visits. The climber may enjoy all the pleasures of new ascents, if only he refrains from searching the records in which a claim of priority has been made, and from making such a claim himself. But man is a vain creature and climbers are not the least vain! The upper parts of the main valley are rich in pasture and a bed in old hay at Chavanis is no bad prelude to an exploration of some of the modest ridges above, whose charms remain in the memory though their publicity value is nil.

Yet another valley opens its door opposite Cogne, the Grauson glen. It gives access to several small rocky peaks and to its own secluded upper pastures, where the legend that edelweiss only grows in perilous places is effectually destroyed. I have picked a bloom there as easily as one can pick butter-cups, but perhaps it is wrong of me to say so. If the head of the glen after it turns east is reached, it is not a very grievous addition to the day to climb the Tersiva. Placed as it is, on the edge of the Italian plain, the view is exceptionally fine, and on a clear day it includes almost all the peaks we have mentioned in this chapter.

Other valleys beside the Cogne valley open south from the Val d'Aosta; they are not for motor folk. The way up to Dégioz in the Valsavaranche is only by courtesy a road. A few years ago I did come down from Dégioz in a carriage, a wonderful affair, very narrow and with an immensely high seat; it was springless, but nothing more adventurous than a walking pace was desired till we reached comparative safety near the main valley. Mercifully one or other of two deep ruts hugged at least two wheels most of the way and allowed us to contemplate what was beyond the outer edge of the road with fair assurance; when the ruts ceased, we walked. A remarkable dog accompanied us. If only genius were transmittable the puppies of this dog would be worth their weight in gold; it licked the horse whenever it was getting hot, it never got in the way, and it acted as a perfect liaison between our party and the driver when we cowered in separate shelters from an appalling thunderstorm. I cannot describe its breed.

The next valley westwards is the Val de Rhêmes. There is a road up it, but it is one way traffic most of the way and chains are advisable in wet weather. Moreover the valley runs up to the frontier and its neighbourhood is to be avoided till political changes occur.

I have said a good deal about this district round Cogne because it contains so much that is typical of the Alps as a playground. The other centres in the Graian Alps can be only briefly mentioned. Now that the road runs through, and not only up to Val d'Isère, that village will develop rapidly the the things that motorists require. At the same time it will continue to provide for the visitor who wants them, places where he can enjoy upland pastures and summits fairly easy to attain, without fear of disturbance from a tourist crowd.

Bonneval is more austere than Cogne or Val d'Isère and the valley more shut in; There is a fine group of mountains east of it, whose best peaks are the Ciamarella and the three summits of the Levanna, and two or three well-placed climbing huts belonging to the C.A.I. which stands for Centro Alpinistico Italiano, since "club" became a word that should not proceed from the lips of good Italians. This Bonneval district has been a favourite setting for the Alpine stories of M. Henri Bordeaux.

Cérésole is nearly as high as Cogne, but it feels much lower, because of the great wall of the Levanna on the south side. The surroundings are charming and fully appreciated by Italians, whose cars can now reach it. There is one spot I should never fail to visit if I went back to Cérésole; it is 2,000 feet above, on the hunting path that runs northwards up the hillside and takes you towards the Col de Gran Crou. It must be the loveliest camping ground in the Alps and a great favourite with the King, whose suite occupied niches in the rocks that surround it. It has a rich carpet of green and a clear stream running through it. In addition, it is just below the four peaks we looked at from the Victor Emmanuel hut.

Before leaving the Graians I must mention one more peak, the Ruitor, not far from the Petit St. Bernard, simply for the unique view it gives of the Mont Blanc range, which is the subject of the following chapter.

48 (*opposite*)
Lillaz and the Valleille

III

THE MONT BLANC RANGE

WHAT is familiar to all and has been the object of fervent admiration for one or two generations is sure to suffer changes in favour with a new generation that must establish values of its own. Mont Blanc is a good example of this, at any rate with climbers. We can be sure, however, that any eclipse in favour can only be partial and temporary. In the realm of art new creations that are better than the old are always possible. That is not so with mountains; new fashions of regarding them and using them as playgrounds may arise, but not new mountains. Not while the earth remains fit for human habitation can any new peaks appear in the Alpine chain which can rival the supremacy of Mont Blanc. To a supremacy in height—and in the case of mountains height has always been a measure of greatness—it adds supremacy in beauty of form and drapery of snow and in its setting among surrounding peaks, as well as unrivalled variety of mood and aspect. Despite its mild appearance it is the most terrible of all in storm.

To climb Mont Blanc was a mad and hazardous adventure for three-quarters of a century after Saussure's ascent. The Chamonix route may have become "a dull snow grind" for some who regarded it through *fin de siècle* spectacles; the routes up the Brenva face are hardly that, even for present-day experts. In any case Mont Blanc is something more than a test of climbing prowess; poets like Shelley are not fired to outbursts of ecstatic admiration by what is commonplace, and when you see it for the first time as you come over the Col des Montets in a car or over the Col de Balme on foot, or as you may see it driving up from Aosta to Courmayeur, you will experience something of Shelley's enthusiasm and reverence, though you may express it only by silence and not as he did. This is how Dr. Julius Kugy, who is famous both in the making of Alpine history and in the writing of it, describes the southern view: "At one point about half-way up, where this beautiful valley of the Dora Baltea makes its great bend, there was a sudden stir among the company. Something had arisen before us, and it filled the background of the valley. It was neither cloud, nor rock, nor ice. It was all these in one. A fabulous structure of

9   53

49 (*opposite*)
The Mer de Glace and Grandes Jorasses from Montenvers

cloud, rock, ice and snow, a picture great beyond the richest
fantasy, a cathedral borne on giant granite columns, an altar
lit by the glory of heaven, a dome standing brilliant in the
firmament."

Seen as a mere patch upon the map, the Mont Blanc range is
a long, lozenge-shaped group of mountains, separated nearly
everywhere by deep valleys from the neighbouring groups.
Now that walking has had a renaissance under the name of
hiking, it is worth recommending the circuit of the range as
one of the finest hikes in the world. And I propose to take the
reader rapidly round, taking Martigny in the Rhone valley as
a convenient starting and finishing point.

If it is very hot and you have got up a good deal later than
the sun, you may succumb to the temptation of taking a car
or bus up to the Forclaz, which is the pass at the head of the
wide green trough leading westwards, an upward continuation
of the Rhone valley. You will have plenty of opportunity to
admire the way the drivers of great buses take the hairpin
bends on this road; they are some of the worst still remaining in
the Alps. Arrived on the Forclaz you see the flat basin of Trient
some hundreds of feet below you. Half-way down you must
leave the road and descend in view of the grand shattered ice-
fall of the Trient Glacier to the stream, where a bridge takes you
across and sets you at the foot of the ascent to the Col de Balme.

At the Col you enter France, but you may well forget it
with the view of Mont Blanc and his Aiguilles and the vale of
Chamonix spread out before you. If that view does not thrill you
you are better away from the Alps. Your way lies straight down
the valley till you come to Les Houches, four miles beyond
Chamonix. If your feet are weary, you can get into the train at
Montroc station where it issues from the tunnel under the Col
des Montets. There, or at Le Planet, half a mile away, you are
off the through motor road and admirably placed for the
enjoyment of small expeditions and contemplative ease. But
we are now intent on circling Mont Blanc and must push on
to Chamonix.

Glacier valleys open at intervals on our left, inviting us to
explore the recesses of the range. First, above the village of Le
Tour is the Glacier du Tour, and high up on the slopes we can
see the path leading to the hut erected in memory of a great
climber and a great king, Albert of Belgium. At the head of the
glacier is the Col du Tour leading to the Orny glacier and the
Cabane de Trient, a large new building within a short walk of
the easy Aiguille du Tour or the various climbs on the

50 The Aiguilles de Charmoz, Blaitière and Plan

51 The Dru

52 Mont Blanc from near La Flégère

53 Mer de Glace, Grandes Jorasses and Aiguille de Charmoz
from the Flégère path

Aiguilles Dorées. At Argentière, less than two miles from Montroc the dirty tongue of the Argentière glacier hangs down almost to the valley level. In that rather shabby bit of ice there is nothing to indicate the long broad highway of level snow above that runs up to the backbone of the range between two rows of splendid peaks. Only the two end ones show themselves to the valley, like the chosen figures in a chorus, who stand nearest to the audience. On the left the Aiguille du Chardonnet, on the right the Aiguille Verte. The road and railway descend through woods, close to the rushing stream already swollen by the meltings from two big glaciers, till at Les Praz the valley broadens and flattens for the last two miles into Chamonix. At Les Praz we look straight up to Montenvers perched above the Mer de Glace which pushes down in rapidly shrinking breadth between two containing walls of rock. The amazing obelisk which looks as if it must fall on Montenvers, but for the thin attachment that holds it to the Verte, is the Dru, whose conquest, after many failures, by Clinton Dent is one of the epics of mountaineering.

The first broad-topped peak above the Montenvers was the last of the Chamonix Aiguilles to yield to the foot of man. Its twin summits are the Charmoz and the Grépon. The crucial phase of the battle for the Charmoz is typical of this period of strenuous warfare with the Alps at the end of the nineteenth century. The scene is a precipitous gully; its vertical walls are veneered with ice and near the top the constant drip of melting snow has frozen into a horrid bulge of green ice which over-hangs. Venetz, the guide, is clinging desperately to the bulge, while the head of an ice-axe is shifted from the coloured patch in the seat of his trousers to his scrabbling feet. The axe is held up by the arm of Alexander Burgener, transmitting through it something of his immense strength and his indomit-able will. A grand sight he must have been, with his great black beard and rugged frame and features, astride the gully, with his toes on tiny holds nicked out of the ice. And below, out of sight and barely out of range of descending missiles, shivering in stockinged feet and listening to the progress of the fight, the moving spirit of the whole enterprise, the apostle of adventurous ascents, A. F. Mummery.

The Grépon, the right-hand one of the two summits, fell to the same party a few days later. For many years it has been a Mecca for rock climbers and a gold mine for the Chamonix guides. In fine weather there may be a queue twenty climbers long below the famous Mummery crack.

Next to the Charmoz-Grépon peak is the higher and more elegant Aiguille de Blaitière. Both the rocky protuberances on the sky-line to the right have been baptised; the names will tell you to which they belong, Les Ciseaux and l'Aiguille du Fou. Then comes a deep gap in which are the Pointe Lépiney and the Pointe Chevalier, their godfathers being two French climbers of the G.H.M., the Groupe de Haute Montagne, started by a band of young men whose youthful energies had been banked up in preparation for the Great War and were diverted by the Armistice into a long campaign of daring climbs, most of them on these Aiguilles.

The peak beyond the gap is the Aiguille du Plan and the peaklets on its crest have got their names, rather suggestive names; first the Dent du Caïman, then the Dent du Crocodile and finally the Plan itself. That precipice of ice below the Plan and Crocodile was where Mummery with two friends spent two days and a night in a great attempt that just failed. This face of the Plan was climbed by J. Lépiney, Ségogne and Lagarde, and in the course of it they crossed the top of the slope below the Crocodile *at night*, Ségogne having only the point of a knife to help him maintain his balance in the invisible steps cut in the steep ice.

The Plan is the first of these peaks that can be reached with comparative ease from the back. The next, and much higher peak is the Aiguille du Midi, a glorious view-point and for that reason the intended victim of exploitation for commercial purposes. The *téléférique* from Les Bossons to Pierre Pointue and the present terminus, Les Glaciers, is to be extended to the summit of the Midi.

If you have been looking up at the Aiguilles with the concentration they deserve, it must have been from a window of the train or from one of the paths that lead through the woods to Chamonix, for on the road you would certainly have been run into or over long before you got there. One advantage of the road is that it enables you to visit what is for Frenchmen *the* tea-shop of the Alps before entering the maelstrom of tourist activity where the road from the station comes in. The guides' bureau is close at hand in the street that leads up to the village church. There are nearly always two or three highly civilised young men loafing there who will be pleased to take you up the Grépon or the Dru. Shop windows seem to hem you in and dare you to refuse to buy, so that you instinctively put your hand in your pocket as you look at them. If you are a stern hiker who carries most of his provisions on his back, I recommend for shopping a combination of the tea-shop I have mentioned with the Co-op; between them they supply all that a man can want to carry and to eat upon a mountain or in its company, and you will have adopted a good neutral line in politics that uses right and left impartially.

You must dodge the crowds and cross the Arve if you want the best photographs and the best place for mountain equipment; they are both to be found near the station; and two other good things are across the stream, the statue of Saussure and the garden of Couttet's hotel. Saussure is looking at Mont Blanc, though not because Balmat is directing his attention to it; on the contrary, it was Saussure who directed Balmat's attention towards the summit by offering a reward to the first man who climbed it! If any ghosts walk through the streets of Chamonix at night, one of them must be Saussure's. And he will smile at all the changes; a spirit as generous as his could not frown upon them. He saw a meaning in Mont Blanc that Chamonix had never seen; and for a century and a half men have been adding their interpretations to his. Mont Blanc has meant something to poets, artists, climbers, walkers, guides, hotel-keepers and shop-keepers and all who deal in tourist traffic. Chamonix is rightly called now Chamonix-Mont Blanc. Mont Blanc has made it, or rather it has supplied the credit and left to men the choice of how they spend it.

Near the bridge one or two large telescopes are set up on fine days and it is most often at Mont Blanc they are directed. I am afraid it is not the same old fellow in charge of it that was there when this century began; if it were, I should feel entitled to a free look, for it so happened that my first ascent was made after three days of bad weather and I was the only moving object on the Bosses ridge that day and he did quite a good trade which, but for me, he might have missed.

With Mont Blanc and his Aiguilles to look at, one forgets that the valley has a range of respectable peaks, the Aiguilles Rouges, opposite. Immediately above Chamonix rises a steep hill-side with trees reaching more than half-way up and topped by a precipice. Against this precipice, at intervals throughout the day, can be seen the outline of something that looks like a huge bird soaring slowly up close to the cliff. It is not a bird; it is a thing that must frighten any wild bird away, the cage of the *téléférique*, which travels in one colossal, sagging span from Planpraz at 6,000 feet to the summit of the Brévent at 8,500 feet. If ever a *téléférique* is justified, it is this one. For the visitor to Chamonix will have missed the greatest spectacle in the Alps below the snow-line if he has not seen the Mont Blanc range from some high point of the Brévent range. To see a great mountain at its best, you must see it across a deep valley, from its base to its summit, with nearly as much of it below you as above. Till one has actually seen it, it is hard to believe how the stature of Mont Blanc is increased as the height of one's view-point rises on the slopes or summits of the Aiguilles Rouges.

From Planpraz there is a fine choice of paths. If bound for the Brévent, you can take the path or travel through the air; if you like plenty of company the Brévent is your best choice. If you want as much privacy as is obtainable on paths so popular as these, choose the way to the Col du Lac Cornu. The lovely dark lake below the Col on the far side is seldom unfrozen till July. You can continue along the ridge to various points which give you views similar and not at all inferior to that from the Brévent. Another path runs from Planpraz near the tree line to the Flégère; its special merits for photographers have been referred to already in the Introduction. For a fair walker with just one fine day to spend upon this marvellous grand-stand of Nature, this is my recommendation: Take the *télé-férique* up to Planpraz, then the path to the Flégère, and from there up to the Lac Blanc, which has this advantage over the Lac Cornu that you can view the reflection of the Mont Blanc Aiguilles in it. I visited it not long ago in the height of the season and it was not so crowded as to prevent two fair and vigorous maidens of my party diving into its icy waters and finding only cause for satisfaction in them. From the lake it is well worth while to ascend the Belvédère; it is a walk over snow and then an easy scramble up good rocks, where the way is well trodden or blazed by scratches of innumerable nailed boots. From this part of the chain of the Aiguilles Rouges, besides seeing what is seen from the Brévent, you are opposite the opening of the Mer de Glace and so have a grand view of the Grandes Jorasses and the adjoining peaks framed between the Dru and Verte on one side and the Charmoz on the other. From the Flégère there is a choice of paths descending direct to the valley or to Chamonix.

Though it is nearly 10,000 feet the Belvédère is not truly a summit view with far horizons; it is a seat erected for you to see the full majesty of the Alps themselves. It is Mont Blanc itself that gives unique distinction to the view. I can hardly picture to myself now the impression it makes on a person who sees it for the first time; it means so much more if you have

55 Le Petit Clocher de
    Planereuse

54 The Mummery Crack
    on the Grépon

56 Mont Blanc, Aiguilles and Grandes Jorasses from above
the Lac Blanc

57 Blaitière, Ciseaux and Fou

climbed it; so, climb it if you can. Many must go to Chamonix and long to do so and have to go home with the longing unsatisfied. Those who have not experience of high snow mountains must go with guides or with friends who have, and guides are expensive, while most of the climbing friends will be enticed by the Dru or the Grépon or the Requin and regard Mont Blanc as a treadmill job unworthy of their skill. It is a mistake to make the ascent till the system has had some acclimatisation to high altitudes on one or two other ascents above ten or twelve thousand feet; the density of the air on the summit is about half that at sea-level and it is an exceptional man that suffers no effects, varying from headache to prostration and nausea, if he goes up Mont Blanc quite untrained.

What anyone can do at small cost and in any company, including his own, is to go up to the Tête Rousse hut at the foot of the Aiguille du Goûter and spend the night there, at just over 10,000 feet. Let the other people have their supper first, as the sun is sinking; they will be starting early for Mont Blanc and will want to get to bed. Your reward is here. Wrap yourself up as you would to watch a football match on the coldest day of winter, then go outside and sit down to view the pageant of sunset performed in the best setting in the world. Do not go in till night has taken all the colour from the rocks and you have seen the crest of the Aiguille de Bionnassay shining above their dark silhouettes with a strange unearthly radiance that might belong to a soul that is released from earth, yet lingers to watch over it.

The hut on the Grands Mulets is as finely situated as that on the Tête Rousse; it has this serious disadvantage that it is perched on a rock and anyone disposed for contemplative pleasures finds it hard to get away from the various offences that needs must come in the immediate vicinity of a crowded hut. For those who do not want to take one of the more strenuous routes up Mont Blanc, an ascent from the Tête Rousse with a descent by the Grands Mulets is a very good combination. The ascent of the Aiguille du Goûter lies up one or other of the well-marked ribs of broken rocks that run up the face. There is something like a path if you follow the easiest way, which crosses a broad couloir about a third of the way up, and here you must hurry, for it is not good to meet a rock, even a small one, on its way from a spot it has long occupied on the upper part of the face to a new resting-place two or three thousand feet lower, and this couloir is the highway that they choose. From the top of the Aiguille to the Dôme du Goûter is just a grand walk; I know no ridge in the Alps connecting peaks of such a height where a man's attention can be so safely allowed to wander from the path he treads to the prospect that is opening round him. From the Dôme a broad slope leads gently down to the Col du Dôme where the Chamonix route is joined, just before reaching the new hut which has replaced the old comfortless Vallot hut. The old hut may have had a slight sentimental value for Chamonix; it will be unregretted by foreign climbers. It was a cheerless place. A score of shivering unshaven people might be crowded into it without the heat of their bodies being able to melt the snow upon the floor. It did, however, save the lives of men who could not have survived the storms outside, so let us write an epitaph:

> Gone is the haunt of men hirsute,
> That never thawed a frozen boot,
> Where dawn, however wan, was "*gut*;"
> The hut is razed, we raise the "*Hut.*"

It is difficult to believe that a climber as good as Charles Hudson should have descended from here more than a thousand feet to the Grand Plateau in order to complete the ascent of Mont Blanc by the Corridor and the Mur de la Côté on its far side, rather than attempt the ridge of the Bosses du Droma- daire which is straight in front and has been the usual route for over seventy years. On the other hand those broad sloping ledges of snow that lead up from the head of the Grand Plateau between and above the two bands of rock opposite are the ways that were chosen for the first ascent and for Saussure's; they have long ago been condemned and forbidden to the guides of Chamonix as too dangerous! Saussure was lucky, for a great avalanche which might have swept his whole party away fell in the night while they were trying to forget their fears in sleep near the edge of the Grand Plateau—fears of imaginary, not of real dangers, of deadly cold, of the mysterious malaise now known to be the natural result of height combined with injudicious diet on men unacclimatized to high altitudes, of the collapse into the bowels of the glacier of the whole party through the melting by body heat of the snowy floor on which the tent was pitched. Most of the real dangers on these easy ways up Mont Blanc arise from carelessness and ignorance. Dislodged rocks, falls into crevasses, failure to read weather signs and estimate their effect upon conditions will continue to claim victims on routes free from technical difficulties. I

58 L'Aiguille du Midi

dare say quite a number of people who get out of the *téléférique* at Les Glaciers do not realize that the only place where an experienced party is in unavoidable danger is on the path within a few minutes walk of the station where the Aiguille du Midi has scattered its messages of warning in the stones that have fallen from above.

Before continuing our circuit of the range from Chamonix, the alternative of cutting through the middle of it over the Col du Géant is worth considering, even for the hiker. At present the Col de la Seigne, where the line we are tracing round the high mountains cuts the Italian frontier, is closed. Damn Fascism if you like, but it won't open the pass, and a considerable detour by the Petit St. Bernard will have to be made to enable the proper route to be rejoined at Courmayeur. The passage of the Col du Géant is rather more than a simple walk and it is not a walk at all for a man alone. I do not mean that an able-bodied man could not do it; it is not at all difficult, any more than walking across a pond where the ice is known to be too thin to bear safely is difficult; it is just foolish. A man who crosses a large extent of snow-covered glacier alone, if he has any consideration for the friends whom his disappearance in a crevasse would certainly inconvenience and perhaps distress acutely, is compelled to pay great attention to his steps; this constant preoccupation with the ground immediately in front is monotonous and tiresome and prevents the full enjoyment of his surroundings; and in the case of the Col du Géant those surroundings are worth looking at. No pass in the Alps has grander sights to offer. That is why a man who crosses it for the first time alone is a fool. The way lies beside the Mer de Glace for some distance after leaving Montenvers, then over the ice to the ice-fall, the frozen Niagara of the Géant Glacier, which begins below the Requin hut. It is on this next stage which lies over the snow-fields to the Col that a man should be roped to others. On the Col is the Rifugio Torino, a small hotel excellently kept by the Italian Alpine Club. From the Col the way goes down easy rocks and then a path to Courmayeur.

Having suggested this alternative, I come back to resume the full circuit that was planned. Our next objective is Contamines in the valley of the Bonnant and at the foot of the Mont Joly; our sleeping place after Chamonix will depend on the time we reach Contamines and our condition on arrival. There are so many ways of getting there. First by train, car or footslogging to Les Houches, four miles down the valley. An

10

intelligent walker can avoid the road and keep on the south side of the river. At Les Houches the valley bends to the right and descends rather steeply through a gorge to Servoz, where the path over the Col d'Anterne begins, and then to the wide level stretch which contains Le Fayet, where the narrow-gauge railway ends and the rush begins for carriages labelled Paris. The lame, the lazy, and those who believe that energy is made to be conserved will take this line and a funicular from Le Fayet up to St. Gervais, or they will drive all the way to Contamines. The wise expenders of energy will make for the broad depression on the sky-line above Les Houches, reaching it at the Pavillon Bellevue or the Col de Voza, which is some 300 feet lower. The tempter will have one last shot at them, for there is a *téléférique* which offers to hoist them to the ridge a little above the Pavillon. It meets here the cog railway that runs from St. Gervais to what a visitor from Eire would call an unfinished terminus at nearly 9,000 feet. You reach it as you emerge, or, if you are in the third carriage, before you emerge from a tunnel and see the whole length of the French Bionnassay Glacier far above and far below you and accessible also at your present level by a path along the hillside. The inn on the Tête Rousse is only an hour and a half's walk from the terminus.

At Chamonix the prudent traveller will have secured a copy of the admirable map by Charles Vallot called *Tour du Mont Blanc*; the scale is almost exactly one inch to the mile and it is quite up to date. This map will show paths descending from the Pavillon Bellevue or the Col de Voza to the chalets of Bionnassay and on to Contamines. The valley on the left beyond the Bionnassay valley is that which contains the French Miage Glacier. The Col de Miage is not often crossed; apart from present frontier obstacles I think the crevasses on the Italian side below the Col might be very troublesome in a rather snowless year, owing to shrinkage of the ice since early crossings were made. There is a hut on the Col where you will hope to sleep if you have designs on the Aiguille de Bionnassay or better still, on the whole ridge that contains it and connects it with the Dôme du Goûter and Mont Blanc. Anyone who plans this grand expedition will know about the cornices he may expect to find; they are generally big enough to throw a shadow on the white wall, which betrays their existence to those who admire this exceptionally graceful mountain from below.

A very short way beyond Contamines a big path starts from

the road up to the Trélatête hotel at the foot of the Trélatête Glacier, a good starting-point for the various climbs on the Dômes and Têtes and Aiguilles that rise from it. This end of the Mont Blanc range is much less frequented than the Swiss end; indeed it is not so many years since I found that the simplest and quickest pass from Trélatête to the Chalets of La Lex Blanche was unmarked on any map and not mentioned in any guide; the only record is decently buried in a journal, so it awaits discovery again by any climber at Trélatête who likes exploration and is confident of dodging Italian sentries on the way to Courmayeur. The name I thought of for it was the Col Moyen Age, seeing it is akin to the name Miage and because it is suitable for climbers of middle age. Lex means a meadow shut in by hills. The name *La Lex Blanche* is the correct name of the valley, not *L'Allée Blanche*.

Now at Contamines the circumambulator of Mont Blanc must take thought for the coming night. If the day has already advanced to an hour that may fairly be included in tea-time a prudent traveller should hesitate about proceeding that evening beyond Nant Bourrant; having tried them I cannot recommend the slopes above Les Mottets in the dark, particularly if the darkness has the soupy thickness produced by the addition of mist. The plutocrat, posing as a hiker, who alights briskly from his car where the road stops at Notre Dame de la Gorge, with several hours of daylight in hand, may confidently take the path. It is a short mile to Nant Bourrant where a choice must be made. In the expectation that Italy will soon discover that an open frontier is really better than a closed one, I take Les Mottets for the sleeping-place. The Col de l'Enclave is the shortest way to it. Your map shows you how to reach the Lacs Jovet and from there you must judge the best way of dealing with the stony slopes that lead up to the col, and the somewhat kinder slopes down to the stream by which Les Mottets lies; it is on the far side, but in daylight you will scc a bridgc, at night you may or may not takc comfort from the knowledge that one exists.

There is not much view on the way and the upper reaches of the broad green valley up which you have come are rather grim and desolate as you approach the ridge, either at the Col de l'Enclave or at the usual pass, the Col du Bonhomme, where you must keep up again to the left to the Col de la Croix du Bonhomme. From it, if the Col de la Seigne on the frontier is closed, you must descend straight to les Chapieux and leave Les Mottets alone; if the frontier is open, you turn up again

to the left from the Croix du Bonhomme over the Col des
Fours, where you are rewarded by a very fine view before
descending to Les Mottets. At les Chapieux you find the road
again and can be driven down to Bourg St. Maurice and over
the Petit St. Bernard. All day the scenery has been quieter and
more pastoral than the magnificence of the Chamonix valley,
a very good interlude to rest your powers of appreciation
before the splendours of the day to follow.

Let us begin that day well by assuming that you have slept
at Les Mottets in anticipation of nothing more alarming across
the frontier than a perfunctory question about the contents of
your rucksack and the transfer of a cigarette. The path meanders
over pastures in which small torrents have ploughed many
ravines. Above, on the left front, is a rather fine glacier, a
neglected member of the huge family nourished by Mont
Blanc. Its name the Glacier des Glaciers suggests that it came
as an almost unwanted addition, and its surface looks as if it
was intended to be smooth, but actually is like that of a bill
stuck on a door studded with big nails; the water-scored slopes
that lead up to it are the sort that a climber competing for a
peak would wish his rival to traverse in the early morning.

From the Col de la Seigne we look down the great trough
that runs all along the south side of the Mont Blanc range.
The southern wall of the trough has been breached at Courmayeur by the impetuosity of the torrents from the far higher
northern wall, and so the original drainage schemes of nature
have been completely changed. Geologically speaking the
Monarch of the Alps is quite an upstart and has behaved as
such! The view of this side of the range is a fine contrast to
that from the Col de Balme down the valley of Chamonix. In
both cases Mont Blanc is the dominating personality; perhaps
that is why the contrast is so marked, for we see here a very
different Mont Blanc. At Chamonix it has the beauty of an
aristocrat of the north, serene, majestic, a position assured by
a long untroubled reign. Here it has a dark gipsy beauty, a
wild disordered appearance that makes us feel that cataclysmic
forces are still alive within it. And all around are strewn evidences of a similar disorder. Two glistening grey pyramids
of rock close to us, the *Pyramides Calcaires*, are clearly violating
the geological habits of the district in standing there. And
further down the valley at Purtud is evidence of far more
recent violence. When I was there after the War there was a
delightful stretch of wood and green sward in front of the
hotel. In November 1923 it was suddenly obliterated. I wonder

60 The Fauteuil des Allemands and Mont Blanc
from the Chécroui Alp

61 The Grandes Jorasses and Italian Val Ferret

62 Mont Blanc from the Pointe Percée

if the man who was in the hotel at the time often dreams about it. An enormous mass of rock—I believe it was estimated at 4,000,000 cubic metres, broke off from the upper part of the Peuteret ridge and fell down on to the Brenva glacier spreading over a huge area near the hotel in a chaos of rocks to a depth of twenty feet. The extreme edge of the avalanche came past the hotel, parting on a small ridge above it, so that only a single block came through the wall!

The absence of "civilisation" in the shape of railways, *téléfériques* and motor-cars heightens the contrast with the Chamonix valley. Climbers too are far less numerous; there is no Montenvers. You cannot easily forget, as you look at those wonderful Aiguilles of Chamonix, that every point on them has been climbed and has its label and its price. You look at those elegant extremities of the range, the Charmoz and the Grépon, as you might at the ankles of Miss Sofrisky, which have been insured for 50,000 dollars apiece. Most of the points you see from La Lex Blanche have also been climbed, but there are no evidences of it. Even those fine summits immediately above as one descends the valley to the Lac Combal, the Aiguille des Glaciers and the Aiguille de Trélatête are climbed far less frequently than those that surround the numerous huts at the other end of the range, and if you tackle the interesting problem of finding the best way over the gap between them you are not likely to find traces of any recent crossing, much less any other party on the upper snows.

The great bank you see on the far side of the huge puddle which used to be the Combal lake is the moraine of the Italian Miage Glacier. If you climb the bank and look up the long, straight, desolate avenue of stones which forms the surface of the glacier and compare it with the Mer de Glace over which a dozen parties may be picking their way, you are conscious of how much the human element can modify the effect that mountains have on us. Somewhere along those miles of stone-covered ice there is probably a party, for it is the way to both the huts that are used for the two routes up Mont Blanc most often taken from this side, the Rifugio Sella, which in some seasons is by no means easy of access, and the Rifugio Gonella, formerly the Cabane du Dôme, on the easily accessible rocks of the Aiguilles Grises above the Glacier du Dôme.

As we pass the garden into which the rubbish heap at the end of the Miage Glacier has been converted, we have above us the two smaller glaciers of Brouillard and Fresnay. A glance at these broken cataracts of ice shows that they are not for tourist use. On the rocky ridge that separates them is the Gamba hut; the climbs above it are nearly all long and difficult. The general standard of climbing done from this hut is probably higher than from any hut in the Alps.

At La Visaille, the highest hotel in La Lex Blanche, we come under the tremendous precipices of the Aiguille Noire de Peuteret. From here it resembles a colossal arm-chair with immense solid arms and a high peaked back. It is quite a stiff climb to reach the rather sloping seat, the small hut in which is barely visible. The Aiguille Noire is a mountaineer's peak, not a rock specialist's, for it is the finding of the best way, not the climbing of very difficult pitches that is needed, for stones fall frequently from the back on to the seat. Some of the freak routes taken up it are exceptionally severe tests of a climber's luck, skill and endurance. At Purtud we come to the first place where Italian family parties take up their holiday quarters, and here we are right below the Brenva Glacier and from the path near by we can look up at the whole immense height of Mont Blanc, joined to the Aiguille Noire through the Aiguille Blanche de Peuteret. Beyond Mont Blanc, as we walk through the woods towards Courmayer, we see the summits on the ridge we saw from Chamonix, the Mont Maudit and the Mont Blanc du Tacul peeping over the ridge for a moment till it disappears behind the nearer frontier ridge. This ridge rises in a great wall of seven thousand feet above the valley and gives a magnificent ending to the Val d'Aosta as we look towards it from the bridge across the Dora Baltea which brings us into the outskirts of Courmayeur. Mont Blanc itself is invisible from Courmayeur; it is not with you there as it always is at Chamonix.

All the great climbers of the Alps have been at Cour- mayeur and probably none has learned to climb there, except the many guides it has produced. It is a haven whence men set out for great adventures and return from them. You have left the wild scenes of struggle once you pass its harbour entrance. The turning of the corner out of the deep trough below the great mountain wall, from whichever end of it you come, brings you into a different world. Courmayeur is the beginning of the sunny smiling Val d'Aosta; it belongs neither to the Val Ferret nor to La Lex Blanche.

If Italian nationalism is still asserting itself with violence near the Col de la Seigne, you will have gone down from the Croix du Bonhomme to Les Chapieux, not to Les Mottets, and so by the Petit St. Bernard round by road to Courmayeur.

From there you can make an expedition which will recompense you handsomely for having missed the walk down La Lex Blanche. Cross the Dora Baltea to the old picturesque village of Dollone; it is worth looking in at the famous forge of Henri Grivel, where he and his sons make all the prickly things of steel which help climbers to defeat the slippery ways of steep ice. Then follow the path that leads over luxuriant meadows to the Col Chécroui; you may find a *téléférique*, but it is for haystacks only. From the Col you look straight into the Fauteuil des Allemands, the great hollow on the Aiguille Noire; even Hitler's Germany will not produce a man big enough to fill it. Over the high back of the arm-chair looks the southern face of Mont Blanc. If you go on along the easy ridge the path will take you to the upper chalets of Arp Vieille where you look straight up the deeply sunk Miage Glacier to the ridges of the Aiguille de Bionnassay, and when you have taken your fill of what is spread in front of you, you can find a path leading down to the Lac Combal, well in rear of the sentries lying in wait for those who venture to cross the frontier.

If one tries to think of a climbers' headquarters which is to Courmayeur what Montenvers is to Chamonix, the Rifugio Torino on the Col du Géant is the only place that is at all comparable. Unless you fancy the back of a mule for half the distance, you will have to hoist your weight up 7,000 feet. If you do, you will not regret the effort if the weather has played fair. Take away Mont Blanc and the view would still be one of the best, eastwards over the Alps and along the rift of the Aosta valley towards the plains, westwards on a white world with disturbing chains of granite peaks that make of it a fascinating maze. Mont Blanc is there as well, and not to be removed by any faith held by a mountaineer! A very short distance from the inn the Brenva face can be well seen. In recent years various routes have been taken up this face, all of them long and difficult and none of them safe from falling stones or ice save that which is a continuation of the Franco-Italian frontier ridge and strikes the great north-east ridge of Mont Blanc a short distance to the right of the point on it known as the Mont Maudit.

The way always referred to as the Brenva route is the best known and was taken as early as 1865 by a party whose names are famous in Alpine literature, A. W. Moore, Horace and Frank Walker, George Matthews with Melchior Anderegg and his brother Jakob as guides. Melchior having more than once pronounced the projected route "eine miserable Dummheit"

led brilliantly through the wall of ice-cliffs that will always be
a dangerous and incalculable obstacle to the successful ending
of the climb; above this it is easy to join at various points above
the "Corridor" what used to be the usual way up from Chamonix
from 1827 till the opening of the Bosses route in 1859. Half-
way up the Brenva face an extremely narrow crest of ice con-
fronted the party; they crossed it sitting astride of it and edging
themselves along. Mr. A. E. W. Mason has made excellent
use of Moore's graphic account of it in his novel, *Running
Water*, in which I regret to say the villain is a great climber,
almost the only contribution mountaineers have made to the
list of famous criminals! Mr. Frank Smythe and Dr. Graham
Brown made the first of the recent very difficult routes up the
Brenva face more directly under the summit. The hiker will do
well to have nothing to do with this face, however much a visit
to the Col du Géant may have tempted him to try it.

It is high time to return to Courmayeur, where you have
just arrived from the Col de la Seigne.

If you want company, a four-course dinner and a well-fitted
room, you must stay the night at Courmayeur. If plain living
and a shorter day to follow are preferable, it is best to continue
up the Italian Val Ferret to the Rifugio Elena, formerly the
chalet of Pré de Bar. You will have walked under some
famous peaks before you get there; the wonderful spire of the
Aiguille du Géant now hung with a fixed rope and crowned by
a statue of the Virgin, the Grandes Jorasses worthy to be the
queen of any valley not subject to Mont Blanc, the Aiguille
de Triolet and the graceful white Mont Dolent where the
frontiers of Italy, France and Switzerland meet; and these are
only the outstanding forms in a chain in which every rise that
can be called a peak and every dip that could be made into
a pass has given and can give a climbing party a great day, and
yet has retained much of its inaccessibility and distance from
the tourist crowd. The glaciers that push their tapering ends
into view over sheets of slabby rock are not inviting, nor is
there any sign of broad well-kept paths such as lead you to
the sides of the Glacier d'Argentière, the Mer de Glace or the
Glacier des Bossons. Only the last in the valley, the Glacier of
Pré de Bar wears a look of welcome and spreads out a curious
flat mat of ice for you to walk on almost at the doors of
Pré de Bar.

This is one of the perfect places. It is situated, like Fafleralp
in the Lötschental, on an eminence which gives you the feeling
of height and freedom and a view down the whole length of

63 The Brenva Face of Mont Blanc

64　The Bisse de Montana

65　The Aiguille and Glacier of Bionnassay

an exceptionally beautiful, unspoilt valley, while at the same time a long vista of splendid peaks invites you to look up at them and finally rest your gaze upon the Peuteret ridge of Mont Blanc. The pastures that surround it are often still uncut in early August and particularly rich in flowers. When I first stayed there a good many years ago, my host also had a special attraction, for he addressed me in accents which I only expect to hear north of the Tweed; moreover he gave me ham and eggs of the best and the *Glasgow Herald* to help me to digest them! Yet his name was Proment and he came from Courmayeur. You get surprises like this in the Alps, particularly in the Italian Alps; I remember asking for a drink of milk near the Teleccio alp, a very remote spot in the Graians and being answered in the language of the U.S.A.

If you have got as far as Pré de Bar without being challenged by a frontier guard, you may be able to pursue your way in peace over either of the two cols called Ferret; the Petit Ferret is shorter, the path is not so good; on the other hand it may offer some easy sliding over old snow on the Swiss side. As you enter that country of peace and freedom, the only so-called democratic country where politics is not a struggle to obtain power, you might wonder how it is that the man who greets you at the first Swiss chalets and whose interests are almost identical with those of your host at Pré de Bar should live under such an utterly different régime. Perhaps Proment's father fought to create the free Italy of 1860; Proment's son may have fought to further a dictator's interests in Spain. Fortunately it is after we get home that we think about these things, not in the Alps. Your worry, if you have one, is whether that place on your toe is going to be rubbed sore by the descent and whether the bus will have left La Fouly when you get there.

La Fouly is the highest place in the Swiss Val Ferret which is a headquarters for comfort-loving visitors. It is very well placed. The path to the Col de Fenêtre comes down close to it and opposite there is a grand view of the Glacier du Mont Dolent and the Glacier de la Neuvaz, with the backbone of the Mont Blanc range above them from the Mont Dolent to the Tour Noir. After every fresh fall of snow it is a glorious sight.

The Swiss Val Ferret is a worthy rival to its Italian namesake, though, except at La Fouly, the higher peaks retire behind high buttresses that rise precipitously above the pastures. Nature's more inhuman side is further away and she seems to yield more readily to man's wishes. The wide expanses of meadow down which the road zig-zags as it approaches Praz-de-Fort are a blaze of colour in early summer before their riches are cut and stored in safety. At Praz-de-Fort we get a glimpse through the woods of the wild stony Saleinaz glen. Near that big, black rock round whose base the glacier curves lies the path to the Saleinaz hut, a favourite with Swiss climbers. The Petit Clocher de Planereuse, less famous but not less difficult than the Dru is just opposite the hut; the glacier de Saleinaz is surrounded by every sort of place of entertainment for the climber, and from its head two interesting passes, neither of them difficult, the Col du Chardonnet and the Fenêtre de Saleinaz tempt you to Lognan and the Col de Tour.

At Praz-de-Fort the circuit of the Mont Blanc range is all but complete; you can reach Martigny, either by train or road from Orsières, or you may strike up the hillside on the left and pass by Champex, a beautiful place beside a lake, now very crowded in summer.

Climbers have their special guides and maps and journals to tell them what to do and what men have done, and the enjoyment of a holiday begins with the planning of it. Sometimes the accumulation of knowledge is sufficient to bury the interest and pleasure of discovery, under the desire and satisfaction of technical achievement; *A chacun son goût*; there is plenty for all tastes in the Mont Blanc range, for rock-specialists and ice-specialists and ironmongery specialists. And besides all these there must be many people, and their number is sure to grow, who neither hope nor care to rival the bigger feats of alpine climbing, who simply want to see and know the High Alps, their snows and summits as well as the pastures below them. For these the range presents exceptional opportunities and so I offer a suggestion for a zig-zag progress through it as well as the hiker's circuit which I have described at length. Any good walker, properly equipped, will find it quite within his powers, if he is with experienced companions, guides or amateurs.

Let the party leave the train at Montroc station. From there go up to the Refuge Albert Premier, a good start which you may offer as an act of homage to that honoured name. Next day cross the Col du Tour and the Fenêtre de Saleinaz to the Saleinaz hut; that is not at all a long day and you will be fresh for the Col du Chardonnet in the morning. Sleep where your fancy suggests on the other side, at Lognan, Argentière or Chamonix; anywhere which will give you a nice restful day to follow and let you sleep at Montenvers. From there you cross the Col du Géant, and if you can possibly spare the time, spend the evening there. Remember that time spent looking at the mountains is quite as profitable as time spent scrambling on them. In one day or two—much must depend on the time and energy you have in hand—descend to Courmayeur or Purtud and go up the Miage Glacier to the Rifugio Gonella on the Aiguilles Grises. Next day ascend Mont Blanc and go down to Chamonix. In the Alps man proposes, weather disposes, and weather may have wisely intervened and imposed upon you one or two days of rest which you never contemplated; such interventions refresh our powers of appreciation as well as replenishing our stores of energy so that we are fretting to be off again. If the weather is perfect and your condition in accord you may do it in a week, and it will be one of the longest and best in your life!

There is a lovely bit of Savoy, north of Chamonix, which is quite alpine in character and, except for Finhaut on the Chamonix–Martigny railway and Champéry below the Dents du Midi, almost unknown to English people. The splendours of the Mont Blanc range naturally divert from it the attention of foreign visitors. The glaciers are small, only a few summits pass the 10,000 mark, but the valleys are full of beauty, great stretches of their green floors being studded with the two star blue gentians, verna and bavarica. The Buet and the highest of the nine Dents du Midi are easy ascents, with views that are justly famous; the Tour Sallières and the other eight Dents du Midi are climbs, some of them difficult. Whether you come to climb or not, you should see the Salanfe basin from which they rise; its praises were sung long ago by Emile Javelle and he has not exaggerated its charm.

The district abounds in attractive passes which are traversed by paths; the Col d'Anterne, the Col de Tanneverge, the Col d'Emaney are three of many. For a climber, apart from scattered small peaks of special interest, there is the chain of the Aiguilles Rouges; it will take him a very long time to exhaust the rock climbs to be made on them, both from the Chamonix side and from the small hotel Bérard, two hours walk from Vallorcine. Finally, there are walks upon and beneath the mountains above Sallanches, the Pointe Percée, the Aiguille de Varens and the Pointe de Colloney, all three of which may claim to show the finest full length picture of Mont Blanc, fourteen thousand feet from base to summit; not a bad picture for our last of him.

IV

THE BERNESE ALPS

It is appropriate to pass from the Mont Blanc Range to the Bernese Alps, because at their geological birth the two were one. By an accident they have been separated by a deep valley, now part of the Rhone Valley, where a northward-flowing stream sawed its way back through the range of which they were parts.

In one respect the Bernese Alps are pleasanter than all the others which form the subject of previous and succeeding chapters; they contain no political frontier. You may cross any pass or any peak and no one will question your right to do so. That does not mean there are no differences in the people; far from it. You may hear nothing but French talked as you leave the village and ascend the valley or the hillside in the morning, and nothing but German when you reach your quarters for the night on the other side of the mountain. If you enter any church in the Lötschental, you can see at once the folk there are devout Catholics. Cross any of the passes that lead northward and you will find yourself among Protestants who thoroughly deserve the name. These differences increase one's admiration for the political sense which gives the same liberty to all and secures in return the same remarkable devotion to their country.

Even in the days when the tourist invasion of the Alps was only beginning, honesty, cleanliness and a measure of prosperity were characteristic of the Bernese Alps, apart from the southern slopes really belonging to the Rhone Valley which have been less favoured by Nature. In most parts of the Alps in those days cleanliness was not next to godliness; it was nowhere. In Dauphiné, for example. What more convincing evidence is needed than that of Whymper's guide: "As to fleas, I don't pretend to be different to anyone else; I have them." And in the Graians, John Ormsby, who claimed to a connoisseur, maintained that for voracity, vigour and intelligent organisation of attack, the fleas of Valsavaranche had no rivals, even among Arabs or Spanish smugglers. Now, in almost every part of the Alps, cleanliness is near to godliness and in some places a good deal above it.

66 The Oeschinensee and Blümlisalp

67   The Märjelensee at the Edge of
the Aletsch Glacier

The line of the Lötschen Pass with the Lötschberg tunnel beneath it, divides the Bernese Alps into two distinct portions, both full of attraction but different. Let us consider first the western portion, which is much less familiar to English people than the eastern, the famous Bernese Oberland.

The lay-out is simple; a line of peaks with short steep valleys descending to the Rhone Valley and gentler slopes with more sub-alpine valleys on the north. The line of peaks is broken into five masses by four gaps. The first mass rises in an immense rock-wall right above the Lötschen Pass; this is the Balmhorn; it is much higher than the others, which are all between 10,000 and 11,000 feet. The Gemmi Pass separates it from the second mass, the Wildstrubel. Between this and the third mass, the Wildhorn, is the Rawyl Pass from Sion to Lenk. West of the Wildhorn comes the Sanetsch Pass from Sion to Gsteig and Gstad; then we come to the Diablerets. Here the main watershed bends nearly south to the gap called Pas de Cheville. The fifth mass is a small chain in itself; I will call it the Dent de Morcles mass, because of the commanding view from that peak, though the Grand Muveran, another of its peaks, is higher.

Winter sports have brought the northern valleys of this district to the knowledge of many visitors. Villars, Château d'Oex, Gstad, Saanenmöser, Zweisimmen are accessible by rail and Adelboden is a short drive from Frutigen on the Lötschberg line. Besides affording splendid ski-ing these places provide fine walks and good mountain air for those who do not hanker after more exciting, higher things. Along the main line of peaks, Nature and the local inhabitants have made admirable arrangements for the good walker and the climber. Not only are there gaps between the mountain groups which enable men on foot or muleback to get easily from places on one side to places on the other; there are all sorts of passes east and west below the peaks, so that you can go from one end of the district to the other without ever dropping to the main valleys on either side.

Say you start from Les Plans de Frénières in the first mountain group. You ought not to leave it without climbing the Dent de Morcles. You go up the beautiful Vallon de Nant to the Col des Martinets, where you come to the Grand Vire, a natural gallery scooped out of the precipitous side of the mountain. You can follow it right along for two hours or turn up nearly half way along it to climb the highest point. There is not a better view in the district.

The valleys on the southern slopes of this part of the chain
are roadless and very much off the tourist track. In such places,
far from either end of a long valley like the Rhone Valley or
the Val d'Aosta, movements of population must have been very
slight, and the resultant inbreeding may perhaps account for
the special prevalence of cretinism, which, like the disease often
associated with it, goitre, is due to an abnormality of the thyroid
gland. Goitre was sometimes valued as it secured exemption
from military service, but a *crétin* is just horrible, an idiotic and
often obscene creature, hardly human. My first meeting with
crétins was in this district, and I shall not forget the occasion.
I was on a week-end expedition with a young Englishman of
eighteen and a German slightly older who were living in the
same pension as myself at Lausanne. We had reached a col
between 8,000 and 9,000 feet to the west of the Grand Muveran
and were about to descend the southern slopes to the Rhone
Valley and come home by train, a typical Swiss week-end trip.
There was a path marked on the map, but Nature does not
always conform to the map. It was October and we saw a long
slope of snow where the path should have been; it had been a
fine night and it was frozen hard. I was the only one who had
an ice-axe and I began to cut steps down. Suddenly I heard a
startled Damn! followed by a rapid diminuendo of damns and
saw the English youth flying down the slope in a sitting position, which he maintained for some time before turning over
and losing all control. Near the bottom of the slope he came to
a sort of bank, went through the air for several feet, and
came to rest beside a boulder. To our surprise and intense
relief we heard a faint cry. It took three-quarters of an hour to
cut down to him. He was sitting up when we reached his level.
To save time I asked the German to go to him while I cut to
the bottom of the slope, which was a better line than straight
below where he had fallen. A minute or two later I heard the
German shouting. He was one of those people who through
no fault of their own feel faint at the sight of blood and certainly the face almost completely covered by blood from a
severe cut in the head was an extreme test. He went down the
steps I had cut and then hurried on to find help in some
village. The injured youth had enough strength to hang on to
me and leave my arms free to hold with the axe. Once or twice
on the way down he felt faint but managed to eat a bit of
chocolate and recovered. In an hour or more we saw a man
strolling about below us and thought he had been sent up by
the German. The German had met him, but he was a *crétin* and

just grimaced and danced about. And by a strange coincidence the next two persons we met were also *crétins*. It was good to reach a small village at last and find sane, kindly folk. The village people fetched a doctor who came up in the evening and dressed the wound; they did everything possible for us. It was my first attempt at telephoning as well as my first sight of a *crétin*. I had to explain the situation through a defective instrument, in a language which I had hardly begun to speak, to an excitable lady at the other end at Lausanne, who refused to believe that I was not concealing a death. Next day we got down to the main valley and drove to the nearest station. I think the incident contains more than one warning of the unexpected things that may happen to inexperienced parties, even when the map indicates a path.

Let us now have a look at the Diablerets group. From Les Plans it is an easy walk over the Col des Essets to Anzeindaz. Here you will find no five-star hotels; it is possible your bed will be on the hay. As compensation there are rare flowers on the slopes just above the chalets and among the débris below the grey precipices of the Diablerets. The Zanfleuron chalets or the Sanetsch Hotel near them is the place to aim for next day. If you aim high you will mount the wall of the Diablerets, which is not as bad as it looks, if you find the best way and along the west ridge to the top; the descent is easy to the Sanetsch Pass.

A less ambitious, but interesting route to Zanfleuron passes below the Diablerets. You cross the Pas de Cheville and a little beyond it take a path that leaves on the right the lake and chalets of Derborence. The path threads its way through thousands of fallen blocks. They come from falls from the Diablerets which strewed the valley for miles down and brought the lake of Derborence into existence. One of these falls in 1714 was ideal from the news point of view, for it allowed one survivor to escape and report on it. His chalet was built against a cliff and a huge rock fell in such a way that it protected it from being crushed, though not from being buried. This man was certainly born under a lucky star. A stream filtered through the overlying rocks to give him water and he had a store of cheese. It took him three months to make a way out and when he reached his native village of Avent he was taken for a ghost and every door was barred, till the priest who came to exorcise persuaded the inhabitants the man was still alive.

The path should lead you to a couloir called La Passée and a limestone wilderness characteristic of these dry bare slopes called Le Cleuson and finally to, if not across, the stream from the Zanfleuron Glacier not far from the path to the Sanetsch Pass.

From Zanfleuron the man who keeps to the highest standard will cross the Wildhorn to the Wildstrubel hut; it should not take more than eight hours. About the same time will be needed by the lower route to Montana. Having made your way over the Col de la Selle you cross a bare plateau, which has been described as a petrified glacier and then strike a *bisse*. The *bisses* are the watercourses on which the Rhone Valley depends to bring fertility to its sunbaked hillsides. If you see on your map a blue line following a contour, it is almost sure to be a *bisse*. They go through tunnels, and over bridges, they cross precipices, sometimes in a channel carved in the rock, sometimes by propping from below or even suspension from above. In difficult country they are exciting things to follow. This particular *bisse* should bring you on your way to the lake of Luchet, and beyond and below this you strike the path to the Rawyl Pass and go up it for a short distance before branching to the right for Montana; or you may cross the Pass and descend to Iffigen or the Wildstrubel hut.

From Montana the Gemmi can be reached by finding and following a *bisse* near the chalets of Plumagy, climbing up a goatherd's staircase up an apparent impasse at the head of the Respille valley and proceeding over the Schneejoch, which is very little lower than the Wildstrubel itself. The Wildstrubel is an easy mountain with a nice pleasant descent to the Gemmi; you will therefore certainly find the highest is the best way and make for the Wildstrubel hut and not Montana the night before, if the Gemmi is your goal. If it is Leukerbad, car or train will take you there from Montana.

At the Gemmi we are under the great mass of the Balmhorn and Altels. The glacier spread over the face of the Altels is the one whose end broke off in warm muggy weather in September 1895 and swept over the alp near the Schwarenbach inn. The ice-foam of the avalanche was carried over the ridge opposite 1,500 feet high into the Uschinental. The wind in front of it carried cows to points 1,000 yards away and 1,000 feet above the spot where they had been lying. Looking up from the Gemmi 4,000 feet below, it is hard to believe that a portion of the glacier could have discharged such a colossal mass; it was estimated at over 5,000,000 cubic yards.

To cross over the Balmhorn is a very different proposition to the crossing of the peaks mentioned above. The ascent from the Gemmi is not difficult; the descent on the east is long and

68 The Bernese Alps from Pilatus

69 The Aletsch Glacier, the
largest in the Alps

70 (*overleaf*)
The Jungfrau in evening light

71   The Kienthal

72   The Balmhorn and Altels

difficult. It is best to descend to Leukerbad and from there cross one of several passes to the Lötschental. The Ferden Pass is perfectly easy and it gives a magnificent view up the Lötschental, the most beautiful valley in the district.

I have described some of the passes south of the main chain. There are passes leading east and west on the north side also; they have this very great disadvantage that the Pennines are hidden and the great glory of any view from a high point in this district is the chain of the Pennines opposite, whose snowy peaks have no rivals in the Alps for beauty and individuality of form.

The eastern portion of the Bernese Alps, known as the Bernese Oberland, is quite different from the simple chain of peaks which is the backbone of the portion just described. It is a very irregular group of great peaks with no single dominating watershed. The general habit of other Alps is to present a dark, bare, straight back to the sunny south and less precipitous glacier-clothed slopes to the colder north. The Oberland is unconventional in having an immense wall of precipices facing roughly north-west. If you start from Meiringen to walk over the Grosse Scheidegg (you can drive as far as Schwarzwald alp), the peaks of the Engelhörner, where Oberland guides and ardent amateurs learn to climb difficult rocks, are the first bit of the great wall. At Rosenlaui the Wellhorn, and at the Grosse Scheidegg the Wetterhorn, tower up in thousands of feet of bare rock. As you descend to Grindelwald the Mettenberg and the Eiger continue the wall up to the Little Scheidegg.

In winter, Grindelwald lives very much in the shadow of that wall, and though it can be depended upon to keep out the sun, the same is not true of the wind. At certain times the warm, dry wind called the *Föhn*, and locally "the old man of Grindelwald," pours down with terrific force over it. It happened once in early spring when I was there. A guard patrolled all night, seeing that all fires were put out, in case they should be blown into the room, and that no one smoked in the street. It blew in thirty windows of the Bear Hotel and carried away a bit of balcony. Its warmth was formerly attributed to its being a visitor from the hot desert of Africa, a sort of wandering simoon; the warmth is almost certainly due to compression when the wind is forced down, as a bicycle pump gets warm when used.

In the Eiger the wall attains its greatest sheer height above the pastures; and its north face has been the scene of recent tragedies to reckless young men competing for Olympic medals for "alpine valour." In August 1936 the bodies of an Austro-German party of four could be seen for days lying or hanging from a piton, where the heroic efforts of the local guides were quite unable to reach them. The comment of a Swiss authority on mountaineering was: "The forcing of the Eigerwand is principally a matter of luck—at least 90 per cent of the latter is required. Extreme forms of technical development, a fanatical disregard of death, staying powers and bodily toughness are in this case details of secondary importance. The incalculable element of chance in escaping stonefalls, avalanches, etc., is so overwhelmingly important that this face-climb lies completely outside the pale of mountaineering, belonging more to a degenerate form of the Children's Crusade in the Middle Ages." It has now been climbed, so I hope the above quotation will not induce some young reader to attempt it.

There are two wide breaches in this great wall of Grindel-wald, through which the Upper and Lower Grindelwald Glaciers descend to the valley; both afford easy access to the passes and peaks above and beyond. They come down lower than any glacier in the Alps, except perhaps the Glacier des Bossons near Chamonix, so low that tourists at Grindelwald are within a short walk of the ice-caves that have been dug in their snouts. Nature seems to have had the interests of the tourists particularly in mind when she fashioned the Oberland. The approach to it is easy not only for the Swiss but for the multitudes who use the international railway junction at Basle. Its peaks are the only high Alps visible from a European capital, Berne, and two of its loveliest members, the Jungfrau and the Blumisalp, display their beauties without insisting on any previous journey up a valley; not like the Matterhorn or Dent Blanche which demand an expensive ride in train or car or a tiring walk out of the Rhone Valley before they will reveal their charms.

It is astonishing with what speed the glaciers of Grindel-wald can be "done," at any rate by Americans. For speed they beat the English hollow! I remember one spring a party arrived very late after dinner and a scratch meal had to be provided for them. Before I came down to breakfast—not much after 8 o'clock—they had risen at dawn, drunk their *café*, driven to the Upper Glacier, laid their hand upon it, which appeared to be the test of having "done" it, driven back and had already departed by the early train to do another place.

Beyond the corner at the Kleine Scheidegg the great wall turns rather more west, forming the side of the Lauterbrunnen valley. The green alps above Lauterbrunnen on both sides, those where the train runs past Wengern Alp and Wengen and those on the high shelf on which Mürren stands provide scenes of beauty that are unforgettable. Commercialism has done something to spoil the Alps themselves with its hotels, its railway, its bazaars and its crowds, but it has canalised the tourist stream and it has enabled tens of thousands to look at things which it is good for man to look at.

At no point does the crest of this western wall of the Lauterbrunnen valley drop below 11,000 feet, nor is there a single way up it between the Eiger and the Wetterlücke the gap to the west of the Breithorn which is not a long and rather difficult expedition. If I had to lead a party that was not a very strong one over it I would choose to cross it at its highest point, the Jungfrau itself, starting from the Rottal hut. The Gletscherhorn, the Ebnefluh, the Mittaghorn and the so-called passes between them are all long and difficult climbs, severe tests of mountaineering sense, as well as of skill on both rock and ice.

I have forgotten! There is one very easy way up the wall—if you can afford it—I mean the Jungfrau railway. At the station on the Jungfraujoch, the present terminus, you will be close to the Jungfrau, with a glorious expanse of snowfield before you to the south and a boundless view over the lakes and plains of Switzerland to the north. Climbers often abuse—and often use railways and *téléferiques*. At least they bring non-climbers into the world above, over which the great peaks preside; they enable them to know the peaks as Miss X from the country knows the great personages who preside at Court when some obliging lady has presented her. And that is something, at any rate to her!

To the ski-er in winter or spring this railway offers a grand opportunity. The broad, smooth Jungfrau Glacier invites him or her to run down to Concordiaplatz, the biggest glacier-circus in the Alps, so flat that in summer the water from the melting snow cannot get away and produces sopping slush many inches deep. The early climbers had nowhere to sleep on the south side of these peaks nearer than the hotel on the slopes of the Eggishorn and they often spent most of the night after a long expedition in trying to find it. The damp cleft near Concordia called the Faulberg Cave was a place to exist in but not to sleep in. There is now a small hotel at Concordia for those who can afford it and a hut for those who cannot. Ski-ers should not forget that bad weather at near 10,000 feet in winter or spring is not to be trifled with, and that they may be weather-bound for some days.

At Concordia one realises that the Oberland is a district of great glaciers even more than of great peaks. The face of the Jungfrau which you looked at as you ski-ed past it rose nearly 3,000 feet above the glacier; the Aletschhorn descends to the trough leading to the Lötschenlücke in a wall of ice and snow that is higher still. But so broad and long are both the glaciers that flow beneath them that the peaks are dwarfed. They do not dominate, as the peaks of the Pennines do, the snowfields at their bases.

The greatest glacier highway in the Alps is that which runs through the heart of the Oberland beginning near Fafleralp and ending near the Grimsel. It fills the head of the Lötschental, rising gradually to the perfect gap of the Lötschenlücke and descends in the same straight line even more gradually to Concordia. For all its innocent appearance it has plenty of crevasses below its surface. You can go straight on continuing in the same line, and still on very easy slopes, to the Grünhornlücke and then you bend slightly to the right as you descend, for the Finsteraarhorn presents a magnificent obstacle to further progress in a strictly straight line. If you are moved to climb it, you make for the Club Hut conspicuously placed a short way up the slope, or for the Hügi Sattel, which is the last gap below the summit in the north-west ridge. If you wish to continue in the great highway you make for the Gemslücke or Rothhornsattel, a gap easily reached in the long south-east ridge of the Finsteraarhorn and descend without difficulty on to the Studerfirn and cross it to the Oberaarjoch and hut. From there you get a glimpse in profile of the north-east face of the Finsteraarhorn on which Miss Gertrude Bell with her two guides fought one of the fiercest two-day battles that has ever been fought in the Alps. She descended with every mountaineering honour save the comparatively trifling one of having reached the highest point. The long straight Oberaar Glacier and two or three miles of path take you to the Grimsel.

This grand glacier expedition, which any party of good walkers that takes sensible precautions with the rope can accomplish, might be done in a very long day; it is far better done in at least two, if for no other reason than to ensure the spending of a night, and particularly the approach and the disappearance of night, above the snow-line, at one of the huts which are dis-

73 The Northern Wall of the Oberland by the
Wetterhorn Group

74 The Lauterbrunnen Valley

75　Near the entry to the Lötschberg Tunnel

76　The Bietschhorn

77 A Rescue Party on the
North Face of the Eiger

78 The Eiger, Mönch and Jungfrau from St. Beatenberg

79 The Wetterhorn from the Kleine Scheidegg

posed at intervals all along the way. On æsthetic grounds, I should stay at the Lötschenlücke; staying at Concordia would divide the distance better. Starting from Concordia, when I was young, it took me sixteen hours to reach the Grimsel, but I climbed the Finsteraarhorn on the way which must have added six or seven hours.

A great feature of the Oberland is the valleys that run east and west parallel instead of at right angles to the main watershed. Such valleys are often full of variety and beauty. It may be due to the difference in the amount of sun the two sides get. The Lötschental is the central one, the beginning of the great highway through the Oberland which has just been mentioned. On the north, parallel to it, is the Gasterental with the Tschingel Pass at its head and on the south is the trough of the Great Aletsch Glacier after it has bent round the Aletschhorn. These valleys separate ridges which are quite different. North of the Gasterental is the ridge of peaks all near 12,000 feet, called the Blumlisalp, which conform to custom in turning a bare, grey back to the south and inviting snows to the north. On the other side of the Gasterental is the hog's back of the Petersgrat. This broad, snowy ridge runs at an almost uniform height from the Hockenhorn above the Lötschen Pass to the Tschingelhorn, where it takes a sudden step up of 1,500 feet before dropping at the Wetterlücke to its old height of 10,500. The Petersgrat can be crossed easily at many points and it has clearly been designed for man's benefit, for from anywhere upon it the Bietschhorn is a glorious thing to look at across the depths of the Lötschental, while the rest of the ridge on which it stands is low enough to let the Pennines be seen over it. The glaciers that have spread themselves over the Petersgrat will deposit you gently on easy rocks at the heads of valleys or slopes that descend into the Lötschental. And these lead on to alps that are most seductive and comparatively unfrequented. Nor is the rock scrambler forgotten. Between these side valleys, rising from the glacier's southern edge, are small rock peaks that project into the Lötschental and can give the visitor to Ried or Fafleralp delightful days. The traverse of the Tellispitze is by no means a contemptible climb.

At the Wetterlücke the ridge above the Lötschental begins to coincide with the arc of high peaks that close the Lauterbrunnen valley. Till you have been there you would never suspect the alarming thinness of the crest of snow which actually forms the innocent-looking summit of the Grosshorn. The gap between it and the Breithorn on the west, the Schmadrijoch,

is the easiest way across the wall till you come round to the
Lauitor near the Jungfrau, but though the easiest it is by no
means an easy pass. There is a wealth of peaks to make the
upper Lötschental a pleasant place for the climber and also
for anyone who loves unspoiled Alpine beauty at its best.
For this valley is unspoiled; you cannot get a car yet beyond
Kippel and even to get it there you have to put it on a train to
get it to Goppenstein! It is hardly worth it for a three mile
ride. So Ried, which is a good hour's walk from Kippel, and
Fafleralp, ideally placed on top of a rise in the valley, an hour
and a half beyond Ried, are both out of ear-shot of a car, and
the number of tourists in these days who can face a ten mile
walk is not too large, nor are they the type that will do anything
to spoil the beauty they have come to see.

The Lötschental offers the climber a double portion of good
things; for the ridge of peaks that enclose it on the south is a
worthy rival of that which runs from the Petersgrat to the
Mittaghorn on the north. And except for the Bietschhorn,
whose attractions are so overwhelming that it cannot escape perpetual attention, the peaks upon it are seldom visited. The reason
is that the long valleys which lead southwards and whose ends
are bridged by the Lötschberg railway as it descends to Brig are
the least frequented and the most desolate in the Alps. If you
want quiet, I recommend the Bietschtal or the Gredetschtal,
and remember to take food with you as well as a sleeping bag!

The easiest pass across this ridge is the Beich Pass (not quite
a bike pass, though it is often that on English lips). It leads to
the Oberaletsch Glacier and Belalp. The drawback to Belalp is
the climb up to it after any glacier expedition. From the Rhone
Valley the climb is more than 5,000 feet; that is all right; but it is
1,300 feet up from the Aletsch Glacier and 600 feet at the best
from the Oberaletsch. When you get there the view is superb.
Looking across at the Weisshorn you understand why Professor
Tyndall, who climbed it first, had his house built here.

The Aletsch Glacier which began at the Lötschenlücke has
made a huge curve and is now below you. On the far side of
it is the hog's back of the Riederalp, another delectable place
—once you get there. The views are similar to those from
Belalp; the difference is that at Belalp there are behind the hotel
some good expeditions which involve no preliminary descent;
at Riederalp there are not. It is a place for gentle walks along
the hog's back, good air, good appetite, ease and contemplation; not a bad list.

I associate the Oberland more than other districts with lakes.

Not only is the big lake of Thun visible from many of the high points, lakelets abound. The largest of these, if we exclude the hydro-electric reservoir at the Grimsel, is the Oeschinensee above Kandersteg. The photograph will give you some idea of the attractions of this lake, but you must enrich it with almost every colour you have seen to approach a true likeness. There are smaller and less famous lakelets that are gems worth looking for. Two are near Fafleralp and the names will give you an idea of their surroundings, the Schwarzsee and the Grunsee, the first a dark beauty kind to bathers, the second clear as crystal, icy cold. And there is one that cannot disappoint the highest expectations, unless Nature has opened, as she occasionally does, some hidden waste-pipe and drained its waters away, the Märjelensee, at the side of the Aletsch Glacier, five miles below Concordia. Choose a day when the sky has given the water and the cliffs of ice and the floating bergs a chance to use and intensify its sunlight and its blue, and I think you will be content with it.

There is one point about the Oberland which I introduce with apologies to this beautiful region. That is its weather, whose character is given away by the size of the glaciers which it produces. You will get many perfect days there, but fewer than elsewhere; I should put the Griesalp and the Grimsel as the two wettest places. I have not checked that selection by statistics of rainfall, for they do not always tell the tourist what he wants to know; a quarter of an inch on seven days is a very different thing from his point of view to an inch on two days.

The Haslital that runs from Meiringen to the Grimsel is the boundary of the Oberland and I might have made it the limit of the chapter. It is usual to include in the Bernese Alps those that rise between the Haslital and the valley of the Reuss, through which runs the St. Gotthard road and railway. They are overshadowed by the splendours of the Oberland. The southern peaks of the group, the Galenstock, the Dammastock, the Rhonestock, and others have not the nobility or elegance of form of the best Alpine peaks; stocky is not an unfair description of them as compared with their great neighbours to the west. The northern part is the Titlis group. The Titlis is one of the easiest mountains to ascend in all the Alps. It was first climbed by monks from Engelberg in 1744, and the ascent may be made from an exceedingly pleasant spot, the Engstlen Alp, which is an extensive stretch of pasture with a good hotel, a lake with trout in it, bathing huts and boats.

There is one spectacle which everyone who visits the Bernese Alps should see before he leaves, if he can possibly do so. I mean the kindling of the peaks at sunrise across the Rhone Valley. Monte Rosa and Mont Blanc have a close race to be first; the Mischabel and the Weisshorn are but a few moments behind; then follows an array of gleaming points so rapidly one loses count of them. It is time we moved across to make closer acquaintance with them.

80 The Eiger, Mönch and Jungfrau from the Lake of Thun

81 The Fletschhorn and Mischabel Group from the Bettmer Alp

82 The Grimsel Pass and Gletsch

83 The Fischer Glac
looking to the O
Aarhorn

V

THE PENNINE ALPS

In choosing the subjects for these chapters I have tried to balance the area covered against the importance of the peaks. The Eastern Alps are the most extensive but the least in height and in the size of their glaciers. The Mont Blanc Range is the smallest in area but Mont Blanc stands aloof in unquestioned supremacy, rising 12,000 feet from the green valleys below on either side. The Pennines are the glorious climax of the main crystalline chain, where it lifts itself in peaks that are higher and more strikingly individual than any other great peak, except the Viso.

In the Pennines, which extend from the Great St. Bernard Pass to the Simplon there are more high peaks than in any other district. At the beginning of this century there were forty-three over 13,000 feet, seventeen over 14,000 feet, and four over 15,000 feet. This was the number on a climber's list and, as you know, the more peaks you can provide for a climber the better. For instance, an active man can bag three or even all four of the fifteen-thousanders in a day; he might even put in two or three fourteen thousanders as well for record-making purposes. To an ordinary man they would all be included in the mountain he thinks of as Monte Rosa.

You might suppose that if the number of peaks over 13,000 was forty-three in 1900, that would be the number still. It is true that we have the good fortune to live in a time when geological changes are slow and that the increase or decrease in height of the Matterhorn in a lifetime is imperceptible. That number of forty-three may have been increased by points that have hitherto escaped notice and have recently been noted, climbed and baptized and so born into new life and passed into official lists. A perpetual menace hangs over the men who want to have climbed every peak in the Alps over 4,000 metres. An enterprising young climber creates and climbs a new point on a ridge that passes the 4,000 mark, or it may be a surveyor who, rightly or wrongly, asserts that a height of 3,999 metres assigned to a peak should be 4,001 and some poor old gentleman has to emerge from an honoured and peaceful retirement to climb again to that alarming height in order to keep his

record free from blemish. The Pic Luigi Amadeo on the
Brouillard ridge of Mont Blanc is an example of creation by
climbing and the Piz Zupo in the Bernina Group of promotion
by re-measurement in this 4,000 metre class. Fortunately
20,000 feet is too high for the Alps and peaks of 10,000 feet are
too numerous for this sort of obsession to be common among
Englishmen. There are more than 750 of the latter and that
is a great number for a man to climb, though I believe it
could be done if he started early and continued to regard
mountains steadily from the statistical standpoint.

Zermatt in the Vispthal is by far the most famous centre in
the Pennines for the number and height of its peaks. They cluster
round it on every side. From Randa, seven miles down the
valley rise the Dom on one side, the Weisshorn on the other,
the highest peaks in the Alps after Mont Blanc and Monte
Rosa. Round the head of the valley is the wide arc in which the
main Alpine Chain asserts its greatest victories over the forces
of decay and denudation. Only in one short stretch, where the
Theodule Pass crosses it, does the level fall below 12,000 feet,
and that drop in height is just what gives to the Matterhorn its
unique qualities of height and isolation. The Mustagh Tower
and other spires of the Himalaya may be higher; even to the best
climbers they may convey a sense of inaccessibility which the
Matterhorn has lost. But they rise from scenes of desolation;
the Matterhorn rises from the meadows, as its name implies.
There is no other peak in the world that lifts its ice-hung cliffs
into such sudden, high seclusion from a pediment that is em-
bedded in green pastures. It is the closeness to civilisation of
this naked giant left standing by itself that makes it so extraordinarily impressive.

What wealth this show piece must have brought to Zermatt!
Hundreds must have ascended it who have never before or
since ascended any other big mountain. So crowded is the
face we see from Zermatt in fine weather that it is a trial rather
than a pleasure to ascend it, for loose stones abound there and
the guides cannot check the clumsy movements of their
charges, though they can and do check their falling down the
mountain scores of times in the day.

The Italian side is much firmer rock and is less crowded. I
have been nearly hit by an ice-axe dropped from the rope ladder
high up on that face, once only threatened by a stone. The hut
one starts from is nearly as high as the Solvay hut intended
for use in emergencies on the Swiss side at 13,000 feet. These
are the highest huts in the Alps with the exception of the

85 Monte Rosa

86 The Matterhorn from Guido Rey's house (near Breuil)

Vallot hut on Mont Blanc and the still higher Regina Margherita hut on the Punta Gnifetti of Monte Rosa. In this last hut I have been asked to show my passport.

However climbers differ in their tastes the peaks round Zermatt can cater for them as regards variety and difficulty. The one thing they cannot do is to secure solitude and peace when you are off them and not often when you are on them. The climbs I have myself enjoyed most are these: the ascent of the highest peak of Monte Rosa by the Crestone Rey above the Grenz Glacier with the crossing of the Zumsteinspitz, a moonlight ascent of the ice-fall of the Grenz Glacier with an ascent of the Lyskamm, a crossing of the Schwarzthor Pass, and a traverse of the Matterhorn, going up the Swiss side in moonlight a couple of hours ahead of the earliest guided parties with a descent of the Italian side and a return to Zermatt over the Breuiljoch. Very good were the traverse of the Rothhorn from Zinal, a traverse of the Täschhorn and Dom and a traverse of the Weisshorn back to Zinal, but these were taken in a good week's tour from Zinal and not from Zermatt. Only a climber who has learned to love walking on mountains before he has learned to climb steep places will agree with my preferences and perhaps not even he; for the value of an expedition depends on the unexpected things that happen and not on those which can be reckoned beforehand.

More exciting climbs than any of these stare you in the face at Zermatt. If you want a long climb on sloping ledges which get more and more difficult, till you only attempt the crucial obstacle because retreat has become unthinkable, Mr. Geoffrey Young's route up the Täschhorn will suit you perfectly. It is the black face that disdains the use of snow powder which you see as you look at the mountain from the village. If you cannot find a rock climber as good as the great Franz Lochmatter to go with you—and that is very likely—you must take with you a good supply of the new machinery for making holds in the rocks where Nature has omitted to supply them.

If you want to know what it feels like to be under fire from missiles for several hours or to be hit by one and then, if you survive, to spend the night hanging on to a piton—or better two pitons, in case the one is loose—the Italian route straight up the middle of the Matterhorn's eastern face will suit you nicely. If you want to combine these excitements with constant and extreme difficulty in getting up and in not falling down the mountain, you will choose the route up the north face made by Franz and Toni Schmidt of Munich.

If, on the other hand, you want a pleasant ascent, not long, free from serious difficulty and giving a grand view, you will find the Rimpfischhorn a good choice. I give it preference because of the beautiful walk up to the Fluhalp past the Stellisee, and because the Fluhalp itself is such a lovely spot. The Matterhorn will seem at its very best from here, but you will think the same of that wonderful peak from half a dozen other points of view!

The view from the Gornergrat, the Mecca of non-climbers, is one of those that is honoured with a special panorama in *Baedeker*; that is a far better testimonial than any I can give, particularly as I have to admit that I have never seen it. Partly because of the crowd, partly because of the absence of beauty close at hand as well as far away (that is not very polite to the possible film-stars in the crowd, but you know what I mean), I should choose some other view-point. To a person who is able to walk a little I recommend the train as far as the Rotenboden above the Riffelberg. Get out there, and if you are lucky you will see the Matterhorn in one of its most graceful poses reflected in the waters of the Riffelsee. You may possibly recognise in the small rock peak beside it (the Riffelhorn), the studio where the famous accident to Whymper's party on the Matterhorn was filmed for *The Challenge*. Then take the good path that runs across the hillside above the Gorner Glacier and descends to its edge and the glacier to the Bétemps hut. Here the magnificent ice scenery of the Lyskamm and the glaciers that flow round it is close to you. If you can afford the time, it is well worth spending the night, that you may see the colours on the snow and ice and on the distant Matterhorn change as daylight disappears. The hut may be rather too full for comfort; your night may be broken by the snores of guides and young or hardened amateurs and by the early starts of parties for Monte Rosa or the Lyskamm. But it is pleasant to lie snugly in your blanket—with luck it may be blankets—watching other people get up and fumble with the stove or glower sleepily at mugs of coffee, and then pull on cold stern climbing boots. And at last the door shuts for the last time, the clatter of nails on the rocks outside dies away and you can turn over happily and sleep till the sun has come to make a further stay indoors intolerable.

If you want a fine walk back, turn to the right along the path to the Grünsee, before you reach the Riffelalp, then across the stream from the Findelen Glacier and up to the pastures above Findelen and below the Unter Rothhorn, continuing to the

Tufterenalp, with all the beauties of the Weisshorn ridge displayed in front of you; and so to Zermatt.

Another delectable place is the small lake with snowbanks at the foot of the Stockje. It is a lovely walk to it, either by the Staffelalp and up the "dry" Zmutt Glacier under the cliffs of the Matterhorn, or by the path to the Schönbühl and across the glacier. Both this lake and the Fluhalp can be visited *en route* if you choose your way of approach to Zermatt and your way of leaving it as you should, by one of the snow passes that connect it with the neighbouring valleys. The Schwarzenberg Weissthor Pass is a most interesting way of approaching Zermatt from Saas; it leads from Mattmark over a point on the frontier where three ridges meet to the upper part of the Findelen Glacier and the Fluhalp. The Col d'Hérens will take you to either of the upper branches of the Val d'Hérens, and the Col de Valpelline to the Valpelline and you pass the Stockje on the way to either. None of these passes is difficult; good walkers in good weather with a rope and some experience, their own or someone else's, may safely undertake them.

Zermatt has been given priority of place in this chapter because it is the metropolis of climbing and of tourist activity in the Pennines. Between the Simplon Pass, their eastern boundary and the Vispthal there is one important valley, the Saasthal. The big thing in this valley is the Mischabel, and it is very big. As in the case of the Matterhorn, it is as hard to say which aspect is its best. When you see it lit by the moon from the Almagell alp you know that its beauty is entirely satisfying, and that is also your feeling when you see it rising above the mists from the slopes of the Laquinhorn or from the Weissmies hut. This is one of the best of huts, which remains in touch with the pastures and is at the same time on the very threshold of the wild upper world. If you stay there and climb the Weissmies on a clear day your memories of it will be perfect. The Weissmies may claim the best view and the best glissade in the Pennines and as far as my own experience goes I unreservedly support the claim. I admit that I may be biassed; a perfect day, a new climb, the whole range of the Mischabel facing me, a little further away the east face of Monte Rosa, in the distance a host of old friends lifting up their faces for recognition to east and west, the Lago Maggiore with its tiny white specks of villas round it shimmering in the heat below. Who could see it all and remain unbiassed?

My one day's walk at Saas Fée, for a man who has but one day, must be the round behind the Egginer; preferably going

up by the Langefluh and across the Fee Glacier while the snow
is firm, and back by the Britannia hut and the path that runs
high above the Saasthal to the Plattje. If you are unable to
resist staying the night at the hut in order to make one of the
many ascents from there, particularly if you choose the interesting traverse of the Allalinhorn, you must go up by the Plattje
and down by the Langefluh. The Sudlenzspitz and the Port-
jengrat are the fashionable rock climbs, a very good fashion
that is likely to last. Cars will soon be seen in Saas Fée. I will not
complain; it is good for any motorist to look up at what is seen
on a fine day from that good shelf above the valley. It is also
good to have been there before the cars came, and to have
walked through the woods to Almagell without fear and with
only the smell of the pine trees in one's nostrils.

The Zermatt valley shares with the valley west of it, the Val
d'Anniviers, the greatest row of climbers' peaks in the Alps.
The row is joined to the main frontier chain at the Col d'Hérens
and begins with the Dent Blanche, the great peak at the head
of the Val d'Anniviers. It continues in the Gabelhorn, the
Zinal Rothhorn and the Weisshorn. Every one of the four gives
a great climb on a great mountain and every one has acquired
a personality that mingles with the personalities of the men
whose names are linked with theirs.

Each of the four ridges of the Dent Blanche has a special
character of its own. The long south ridge is notoriously
temperamental. In its best moods it is as benign as such a
creation of gendarmes and cornices can be, but altogether
repellent if its ice has not been thawed. The east ridge, the
Viereselgrat, had character bestowed upon it at its christening.
It was Ulrich Almer who named it with his comment on the
summit after the long difficult climb: "*Wir sind vier Esel.*"
(We are four asses.) The north ridge, with a more difficult
stretch in it than any of the others was conquered by the
superb skill of Joseph Georges, the irrepressible optimism of
his brother Antoine and the fervent ambition of a honeymoon
couple, I. A. Richards and his bride (Miss Dorothy Pilley).
The bride herself has written nice things of this pair of brothers;
of Joseph worming his way steadily up a fearsome wall where
"an occasional pinch-hold was a luxury," with a drop of 3,000
feet below him and two previous desperate attempts on either
side to tax his strength; of Antoine coming up over the last
horrid bulge, exclaiming as his face appeared: "Ah! *les amou-
reux!*" when he saw the pair sharing one foothold and one
handhold to steady themselves and hold him on the rope.

87 Täschhorn, Dom, Südlengspitz and Nadelhorn

88 The Dent Blanche
from Mountet

89 Saas-Fee: Fletschhorn
and Laquinhorn

90 In the Val d'Anniviers:
Lo Besso and the Ober-
gabelhorn (right)

The west ridge of the Dent Blanche will always be associated with Owen Glynne Jones, a great name in the annals of British climbing in the Lakes and in North Wales. In trying to climb a difficult buttress of rock the leading guide fell back on the second guide and Jones, who were holding an axe beneath his feet, and knocked them both over. The third guide was carried away, but the rope, belayed behind him, broke and the last man Hill, was left. He finished the climb, and was caught by a storm as he went down the south ridge. He remained in a cleft, secured by the rope and his axe till near midday the following morning, lost his way coming down and slept by a torrent, reaching Zermatt late next morning; a wonderful escape.

I have taken the Dent Blanche as a typical example of how a peak adds interest to its personality. The Gabelhorn and Rothhorn are not quite so high or distinguished as the other two, but they are even greater favourites with climbers. The Weisshorn carries off the prize for looks. This perfect pyramid, standing well away from the central chain, draws attention at once, whenever it appears. One face of the pyramid, which overlooks the Zinal valley, is an immense rock wall. To climb it near the centre without falling off or being knocked off requires skill, great endurance and bad shooting by the mountain.

In contrast to this grim wall the Val d'Anniviers offers the long, green shelf that runs high above the valley from Chandolin to Saint-Luc and beyond it. Here a man may escape, if he wishes, from ropes and ice-axes, though he sleep at a hotel nearly 8,000 feet above the sea.

The Val d'Hérens and the Val de Bagnes, two long valleys that run from the Rhone Valley to the Italian frontier, differ considerably in character. The road up the Val d'Hérens does not enter it till it has climbed to over 3,000 feet to the village of Vex. It is then carried for miles along a horizontal ledge cut out of the steep hillside, crosses what has been left by the hydro-electric engineers of the stream from the Val des Dix, and passes through the collection of weird stone-capped pillars at Useigne. Evolena in its lovely green basin, with the Dent Blanche supreme behind it, is the first place in the valley where you are likely to find foreign visitors staying. In either of the branches into which the valley divides at the road-head at Haudères, you are sure to find them, and at Arolla is the nearest thing to an imperial possession which England has in the Alps, an English church. In spite of its great height, I have known people who found this church disappointingly low.

The lower part of the Val de Bagnes is full of smiling villages. All the way up to Lourtier the valley bed is wide enough to allow plenty of room for road and stream and cultivation. Going up to Fionnay and beyond it, the mountains close in; beauty is no longer tamed. You will be wise not to try and take a car above Fionnay. In the long stretch of valley that remains there is only one small, simple hotel, Mauvoisin, perched on a platform with a garden of wild flowers round it, above the narrowest and deepest gorge in the valley; it is a perfect place for the hermit-minded visitor. A nose of glacier, now so shortened as to be barely visible, hangs over the opposite wall of the gorge two thousand feet above. When I was first there the bottom of the gorge was covered with blocks of ice which had fallen from it and one saw at once how disaster might occur and how it had occurred in 1818. In that year a huge mass of ice fell and dammed the gorge, so that a huge lake formed behind it. When the dam burst the flood was so terrible that remnants of trees, cattle and houses were carried miles beyond Martigny.

At the very head of the valley on the east is Chanrion. The name recalls to me a wide undulating plateau in the highest zone of pasture, studded with lakes which are warmed by sun and not chilled by glacier ice. Beside the many ascents to be made from the excellent hut there, Chanrion is the starting point for a glacier walk which is a good second to the one I have spoken of in the chapter on the Oberland. It goes up the straight Otemna Glacier and over the Col de l'Evêque to the head of the upper Arolla Glacier. Be careful here to choose the right point to cross the ridge north of the Bouquetins, the Col du Mont Brûlé. Do not get too much to the right. The other side of the right col is easy walking, *if* the snow is good, to the Col de Valpelline and so down by the Stockje to Zermatt. Allow fifteen hours if you want to enjoy the halts.

I must bring you back to Arolla, for it is the best place in the Alps to begin to climb them. I know people who would say it is the best place also in which to go on climbing them, but that is like staying at home all the time, a thing intolerable to the young. At Arolla you are less likely than in other climbing centres to judge a climb by its standard of technical achievement. Climbing is a means of transport over rocks, snow and ice, just as motoring is a means of transport over roads. For beginners a quiet country road is better than a trunk road and some people will always find it pleasanter to average a modest twenty-five or thirty on such roads than to see what they can

91   The Lyskamm from the Görner Glacier

)2   Arolla and Mont Collon

93   The Zinal-Rothhorn

push their car to do upon the Great North Road or some new autostrad designed for pace. The climbing parallel is obvious.

The whole of the long ridge on the east side of the Arolla valley is a climber's way. In case some reader is moved to tread its crest I will mention that there are three ways up to it on which you need not fear a falling stone, the constant threat of which is to me a vile annoyance. One is the ridge leading up to the Dent Perroc, the other two are the ridges that run up on either side of the Aiguille de la Za. That on the left of the Za is the more difficult; it will give you four or five hours of climbing on good rock on a ridge where no stone can possibly hit you; for some reason no one except my parties ever climb it.

The face of the Za and the Aiguilles Rouges are the popular climbs. On both there are stretches where a rock may descend upon you, either of its own ill-will or because a clumsy climber has dislodged it. On the face of the Za a rather impetuous young climber behind me on the rope embraced a large loose rock, which tried to elope with him into the nether regions. Luckily I was well placed and the careful man behind him had closed up, so that only the rock fell, taking many others with it. We waited for the annihilation of two guides and an Englishman whom we had passed below. To our relief a volley of French oaths and not an ominous silence followed the awful clatter of the discharge. It was not till a reconciliation on the summit took place that we realised all that we had escaped, when the guides said: "*Nous vous aurions mangés, si vous nous aviez tués!*" This unfortunate Englishman had been under fire a few days before on the Aiguilles Rouges and a guide was badly hurt.

Arolla is not quite above tree-line, which is also the mosquito-line. Like other creatures of vicious habits they generally spend the morning in bed and come out in the course of the afternoon. A combination of trees and a stream with an impeded flow is a quarter they favour and the owner of water-rights can do something to divert these undesirables to the precincts of a rival establishment. Horse-flies do not seem to thrive here as they do in other places, though the mules which supply them with food and drink bring up at least two posts a day.

In a late season at Arolla you may find colonies of sulphur anemones in less than an hour's walk from the Mont Collon Hotel and most of the high alpine flowers in the course of a walk past the Praz Gras chalets and the Cascade des Ignes. You can descend from there to the Lac Bleu, one of the best of this exquisite species and, if you are made that way, climb the Dent

14

de Satarme if the feet of many climbers have not yet worn it all away. The lazy and those who make tea will find many pleasant sites across the stream within call of the hotel dinner bell. Arolla is still small and the hills around it are big, so that even if the weather is so fine that it chases every visitor out of doors, it is easy to find solitude. May peace remain with it and the hoot of cars be never heard!

Nothing has been said yet of the Italian valleys of the Pennines. To enter them you must go a long way round, for every pass across the frontier except the Théodule is at present closed. All are beautiful, for Nature has been particularly happy in her planting of their lower parts with trees of many kinds, and in the upper parts she has done much to hide the wastes of stones that intervene between the pastures and the snows.

All these southern valleys of the Pennines radiate from the cluster of peaks that stand at the head of the Zermatt valley from Monte Rosa to the Dent d'Hérens. Monte Rosa is at the head of the Val Anzasca and of the Val Sesia which run eastwards; the Lyskamm at the head of the Val de Gressoney and of the Val d'Ayas; the Matterhorn at the head of Valtournanche and the Dent d'Hérens at the head of the Valpelline.

Cars can ascend all these valleys to the highest villages except in the Valpelline and the Val d'Ayas. In the Valpelline the road ends at the village of that name and there the valley divides. One branch goes up to the great pastures at By which lie at the feet of two well-known mountains, the Vélan and the Grand Combin, and no hotel has yet been erected there in their honour. An early memory of these two may be an encouragement to someone in similar case to mine. The Vélan is a very easy mountain from the Cantine on the Great St. Bernard Road. It was the first mountain I attempted with the first pair of boys I took out to the Alps. It is 12,500 feet high and we failed because one of them had mountain sickness 1,000 feet below the top. He was one of the first party to reach 27,000 feet on Everest in 1922, and no one knows how much above that in 1924. Two days later we crossed the Grand Combin, which is much more difficult and 1,500 feet higher.

The main branch turns east at Valpelline and portions of the old path up it are cobbled, a trial to sore feet, especially in descending. Easy attractive passes lead from the upper parts through a complicated array of small peaks into the Val St. Barthélemy and the Valtournanche. The elegant little peak called the Punta di Cian and the lake below it will amply

reward the traveller who chooses these by-ways in preference
to highways.

A delightful way of seeing the upper parts of these Italian
valleys is to cross from one to another by passes at their head.
The Col de Valcournera will take you direct from Praraye at
the head of the Valpelline into Valtournanche, either to that
village or to Breuil. Hydro-electric works have invaded the
vast amphitheatre of lakes and pasture where one could
wander and gaze at the Matterhorn and the wall that runs south
from it crowned by the Dent d'Hérens, the Jumeaux de Valtournanche and others. It would be a grand playground for a
climber if only he had a head no falling rock could split!

One great figure is no longer there, Guido Rey, the most
fervent, as well as the most eloquent adorer the Matterhorn
has ever had, and there have been many. He built a house near
the tree limit a little above the valley bed at Breuil where he
could look up at his beloved Cervino and his scarcely less
beloved Pointe Blanche. It is the point at the end of the delicate
snow crest which precedes the second drop in the ridge of the
Dent d'Hérens connecting it with the Matterhorn, insignificant
for you, but not for him.

From Breuil it is a beautiful walk of five or six hours to
Fiéry at the top of the Val d'Ayas. If you are there in September the small hotel may be empty. Its only occupant when I
first visited it was a wild-looking individual who said he was
inventing a machine and who drew diagrams in pencil on the
table-cloth as long as the black marks showed on it. From
Fiéry the mule path over the Bettafurca will lead you easily
to Gressoney where you come in contact with the road and
what it brings. Between the heads of these last two valleys at
a height of nearly 12,000 feet is the Quintino Sella hut below
the Felikjoch, the only place where I have found stones expressly
provided for pillows. I speak of long ago.

Gressoney is full of Italians in the summer. Queen Margherita used to be a frequent visitor and set a fashion which has
been wisely followed. Here we are in the last of the valleys that
run south. The Val Sesia, next to it, descends east to Varallo. It
can be reached over the Col d'Olen where there is a hotel at
9,000 feet, or in greater seclusion over the Corno Bianco or
much more ambitiously by going up to the high Gnifetti hut
beside the Lys Glacier and crossing the Sesiajoch. Do not be
deluded into the belief that the descent of this pass is safe or
easy because two English ladies with a single guide accomplished it without disaster in 1869.

The Val Anzasca is the last of the Italian valleys of the Pennines. It has all the rich beauty of the others, and it has more; for at several points on the long road down to Piedimulera on the Simplon railway you can see the east face of Monte Rosa, the greatest glacier wall in the Alps; Nature has made no finer ending to a valley.

To wander from one of these lovely Pennine valleys to another, sometimes by easy paths, sometimes by passes far above the snow-line is to have the best of both Alpine worlds, the world of grass and cows and flowers and clear streams and the world which makes a man feel he is only there by kind permission of the elements.

94 Täschhorn and Dom from Egginerjoch

95 The Aiguille de la Za from a
ridge of the Douves Blanches

96 Looking up the
    Roseg Valley

97 The Via Mala

VI

CENTRAL ALPS

COMPARED with the Mont Blanc range, the Pennines and the Oberland, all Alps east of them are minor Alps. There is as great beauty of feature, as great or greater variety and eccentricity of form, but nothing that has the quality of greatness conveyed by Mont Blanc, the Matterhorn or the Aletsch Glacier.

By "Central Alps," as described in this chapter, is meant, first of all, the central chain, east of the Pennines, from the Simplon to the Brenner Pass; secondly the northern chain, east of the Bernese Oberland, from the St. Gotthard Pass to where its summits sink well below the rank of snow mountains in the Vorarlberg hills; thirdly the southern chain, which makes its first appearance in the Bergamesque Alps and Adamello, as far as the line of the Adige, which, with the Brenner Pass, is the line of the railway from Innsbruck to Verona.

As was shown in the Introductory Chapter, these three chains of Alps originated in a main central fold of the earth's crust and two minor folds on either side. The recently constructed trans-alpine railway from Brig to Chur follows the line of the depression between the northern and central folds. We see it further east in the Inn valley below Landeck. The Val Tellina, running east from the head of Lake Como to Tirano is part of the old dip between the central and southern folds. The great extent of the central range will be realised when it is remarked that the whole length of the Engadine from the Maloja or Bernina Passes to Landeck traverses only its northern slopes. One might as well attempt to sample every dish produced by a restaurant that caters for hundreds of different customers in a day as try to do justice to the attractions of these Central Alps in a single chapter, and selection is bound to disappoint many whose favour has been won by some particular district.

Let us begin with the Lepontine Alps, whose highest peak, Monte Leone rises immediately above the Simplon Pass. The crest of the range runs for some distance north-east, above and parallel to the upper part of the Rhone Valley. Though of inferior height to the great peaks west of the Simplon and of little interest to ambitious climbers, this comparatively unfrequented part of the main range offers great attractions to those

who like to get away from tourists and are content with mountains built on a smaller and less formidable scale then the giants
of Zermatt. The peaks round Bérisal and Binn supply the bit
of glacier work and the bit of rock-climbing that are the
essential features of a modest climber's day; the pastures and
the trees and simple hotels supply what is needed when a man
does not want to climb or meet a lot of other folk. The Veglia
alp on the Italian side of the watershed, easily reached from
Binn over the Ritter Pass, is one of the loveliest green basins
in the Alps.

The Lepontine Alps contain what may fairly claim to be the
nodal point of the Alps, and it is curious that the mountains
that provide this topographical climax are quite obscure; I
am sure few readers will be familiar with the Wyttenwasserstock, in spite of its imposing name. It is the passes that cluster
round this part of the chain that make it so important. The
diagram will help to explain this. A_1
is Andermatt. A_2 is Airolo; $A_1 A_2$ is
therefore the line of the St. Gotthard
tunnel and it runs north and south,
underneath the central chain. G is
Gletsch at the very head of the Rhone
Valley; U is Ulrichen a village six

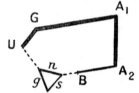

miles down that valley. The road and rail are never far from
one another on this line UGA, and the Furka is crossed
rather nearer G than A_1. The road over the St. Gotthard leaves
this line at Hospental near A_1 and crosses the main chain a little
west of the line of the tunnel. From A_2 to the triangle runs
the upper part of the Val Leventina (the Ticino Valley). There
is a road of sorts from A_2 to the triangle as far as Bedretto (B);
beyond only a path. There is also a path only from U to the
triangle. This triangle has a well-known pass on each of its
sides. g is the Gries Pass over the main chain and leads south
to Tosa Falls, a delightful spot at the head of the Val Formazza,
n is the Nufenen Pass leading west over the main chain into the
Val Bedretto or upper Leventina valley. s is the San Giacomo
Pass from the Val Formazza into the Val Bedretto. It will be
seen that the main chain runs north- east parallel to the Rhone
Valley till it has passed through the triangle; it then turns
almost due east. Another point to notice about this small
triangle is that in it the frontier turns sharply south at right
angles to the watershed. The Gries Pass leads into Italy, the
Nufenen into a valley that is quite Italian in character and
position but politically is enthusiastically Swiss.

Coming from the north by any one of the three "triangle passes" or by the St. Gotthard we shall, if we follow the valley stream to its end, come out at the Lago Maggiore. If we have come down the Val Formazza it will be an Italian shore, if by the Nufenen or the St. Gotthard it will be a Swiss shore. All the three "triangle" passes are traversed in summer by good paths except for a bit of easy glacier on the Gries Pass. If you want to know what they are like before the snow has gone read Mr. Belloc's description of his very gallant attempt to cross the Gries Pass on his *Path to Rome*.

A good indication of the comparatively insignificant character of the Central Alps between the St. Gotthard and the Bernina group is the number of road passes that cross the main watershed. Naturally men looked for ways over the Alps where the mountains frowned down upon them in the least forbidding way. As a rule, the peaks in the immediate neighbourhood of the passes that exist are low, though they may be wild and desolate in appearance, as they are round the Great St. Bernard. No roads have yet been made across the Mont Blanc range, the Pennines or the Bernese Oberland. Between the St. Gotthard and the Bernina group there are no less than four; the Lukmanier, the San Bernardino, the Splügen and the Maloja. The first two lead down eventually to Bellinzona, the two latter to Chiavenna.

Only the Splügen is a frontier pass. This and the Great St. Bernard are the only passes leading from Switzerland towards Italy where the actual pass is not in Swiss hands—and very safe, gentle hands they are. The general character of all these Swiss-Italian passes is a very gradual ascent through a high upland valley on the northern side and a steep descent through far wilder country on the other. The Italian slopes of the Splügen Pass have been particularly difficult to protect from avalanches.

The finest in point of scenery are the Simplon and the two passes on either side of the Bernina group, the Maloja and the Bernina. The Simplon on its long climb up from the Rhone valley provides splendid views of the Bernese Alps; the peaks on either side of the summit rise many thousand feet above it, and the descent through the gorge of Gondo is wild enough to satisfy any taste for sternness in mountain scenery. The other two passes command no extensive views to the north, but there is abundant evidence of the beauties which Nature has bestowed on them in the crowds you see at St. Moritz and Pontresina, and on the roads that lead through them to the hotels on the

Maloja and the Hospice hotel on the Bernina. Visitors did not flock there originally to play tennis and golf and look at one another. In the ten miles from St. Moritz to the Maloja the rise is only about 200 feet; it is the only part of the Alps where I found a bicycle of real use. The descent into Italy by the Val Bregaglia is less gorge-like than most of the other road passes, and the view from the neighbourhood of Promontogno up the Val di Bondo to the glorious granite peaks at its head is a perfect thing to look at before you pass into the luxuriant growth and fruity attractions that fill the lower parts of an Italian alpine valley.

Let us go back for a moment to the Alps between the Lukmanier and Splügen passes, sometimes called the Adula Alps. The glaciers of the Rheinwaldhorn group are generally considered the birthplace of the Rhine. Its waters, for the first few hours after they have escaped from the ice, flow down the almost level floor of the Rheinwaldtal. Then, before reaching Andeer they turn north and, soon after enter the extraordinary deep cleft of the Via Mala, at the bottom of which they roar savagely in sunless gloom for several miles till they emerge at Thusis. In the Rheinwaldtal, the highest village, Hinterrhein, and Splügen with its collection of Splügen Dolomites are good centres for the shier sort of mountaineer. The motorist has brought some increase of noise and smell and prices to these hitherto unfrequented parts of the Alps, and some increase of comfort in accommodation.

In the open valley, just above the southern entrance to the Via Mala, is the village of Zillis, which contains a very old church, one of the few archæological curiosities of this kind in the Alps. It has paintings in the roof dating from about the year 1200, which are still in quite good preservation. One of the panels in the illustration, which might be taken for an alpine Grand National, represents the rush of the Gadarene swine down a steep place to destruction; the incident is one that would appeal particularly to mountain folk.

At Thusis we reach a part of the Swiss railway system which might be called the Winter Sports District Railway, the ring Thusis, Coire, Landquart, Klosters, Davos, Filisur. Within it are Arosa and Lenzerheide. Summer strips it all bare of snow and so robs it of its chief alpine glory. On the east of the Davos valley, separating it from the Engadine is a chain of peaks that rise above the snow-line. The Silvretta group at its north end, east of Klosters, carries some respectable glaciers and climbing huts well patronised by Swiss climbers.

98 (*opposite*)
On the Pizzo Bianco Ridge of the Bernina

100 Cresta Maloja

101 Paintings on the roof of the church at Zillis

99 (*overleaf*)
The Blausee on the Lükmanier Pass

One of the most striking peaks in this wide part of the central chain is the Piz d'Aela, the highest of three dolomite peaks that rise above Bergün on the line over the Albula pass to the Upper Engadine. It just misses being the highest dolomite peak in the Alps, as the Marmolata in the "official" Dolomites beats it by 65 feet. This fine mountain, and its two neighbours built of the same stuff, the Tinzenhorn and Piz Michel, can all be climbed from the Aela hut three or four hours walk from Bergün.

The Albula Pass is more exciting to cross in the train than in a car. The changes of direction are so sudden and bewildering that it is difficult to know whether you are going to Thusis or to Pontresina. At one moment you are in a groove gouged out of the precipice, the next you shoot across the gorge and straight into the mountain into one of the corkscrew tunnels, whence you may emerge going up or down stream. It must have cost a great deal to make this line, but it has probably been worth it, for it carries the greater part of the crowds that are bound for Samaden and the two upper branches of the Engadine in which are St. Moritz and Pontresina.

This east end of Switzerland has always been very "West End" in character, in the prices, leisured ease and luxury, which it offers to visitors. Early in the present century I have seen a four-in-hand drive up to the Morteratsch Glacier with a particularly bright attraction from Paris by the driver's side. The Rolls-Royce that now comes is more serious and more dangerous. A regular summer visitor to the Saratz Hotel at Pontresina told me that on the night of her arrival the waiter put unasked in front of her the particular vintage which she had favoured the year before. Pontresina was said before the War to be a favourite rendezvous for the financiers of three great countries (their ancestors may have shared a country farther east), where they could eat with stimulated appetite and discuss matters of great moment behind a high protecting screen of Alps.

You see what a different crowd it was (and still is), from the crowds of Montanvert or the Gornergrat.

No part of the frontier Alps offers a more striking illustration of the contrast between the snowy beauties of the northern slopes and the great bare walls that extend along the south side of the watershed. The main features of the Bernina group can be seen in two short expeditions from Pontresina. If you drive up the beautiful Roseg valley and walk from the road head to the alpe Ota you get a fine view of the western half. It may induce you to plan and carry out a long and magnificent

day of ridge walking on snow. You start on it by a path that
mounts from the Roseg Glacier Restaurant to the Fuorcla
Surlej, whence you can descend to Sils Maria or St. Moritz.
Instead of that you turn south up and over Piz Corvatsch and
then along the crest over the peaks that surround the head of
the Roseg Glacier, Il Chaputschin, la Mongia, Piz Glüschaint
and the Sella peaks to the Sella Pass. You will have used most
of the twenty-four hours when you get back to the Roseg
Restaurant.

The peak that sends down the great spur between the Roseg
and the Tschierva glaciers and stands up so magnificently by
itself is the Piz Roseg. It is not an easy peak, and may often
demand a lot of step-cutting in a fine season. The well-marked
gap to the east of it is the Porta Roseg. It is easy to reach from
the other side, but the descent of the fearsome wall which
you are looking at, generally hard ice in its lower part, needs
icemanship of a high order. Christian Klücker, the finest guide
the district has ever produced, was the first to bring a party
down it. He drove a stout stick, used for stirring polenta, into
the ice and looped a rope over it in order to let himself down
last over the gaping chasm at the foot of the wall.

The long narrow crest that leads eastwards to the Bernina
is called Monte di Scersen. It is a fine and usually difficult climb.
A rather less difficult and perhaps still finer route up the Bernina
is along the white crest that runs up from the Col to the south
of the Piz Morteratsch. The sharp little point at its end is the
Pizzo Bianco, which is separated from the highest point of the
Bernina by an exciting little jag. A bad place in a thunderstorm
a high exposed ridge like this! Klücker and Norman Neruda
were caught in one up there; Klücker himself has described it.
"The lightning played uncannily above our heads, and there
was no end to the howling and hissing on the Bianco ridge. . . .
There was a roaring vibration round my hat all the while, such
as a strong wind makes passing through a feather, and sparks
were sometimes hanging from its brim, though the hat was
loaded with a quantity of snow and hail."

To view the eastern half of the Bernina group, drive or take
the train to the Hotel Morteratsch and climb in half an hour
up to the Chunetta. The gap to the left of the Bernina beyond
the huge and sometimes impassable icefall of the Morteratsch
Glacier is the Crast'agüzza Sattel, on which the Italian Alpine
Club has built a good hut. The sharp spire near it is the
Crast'agüzza and the lovely snow peaks to the left are Piz Zupo,
the four peaks of Bellavista and Piz Palu. If you sit and look at

them from the hotel with all the evidences of modern civilisation round you this splendid scenery might almost be a part of the vast commercial enterprise that has developed the Upper Engadine. A visit to the upper snows, without any assistance from a thunderstorm, will effectually remove the impression. On the glacier behind the Piz Palu it is easy to forget that tourists exist.

Above the end of the Morteratsch Glacier, as we mount towards the Bernina Pass, we get above the trees into a more desolate region. The Hospice on the pass must be difficult of access in some winters, judging by the depths of snow recorded on the wall, which reach well up among the first floor windows. Not many years ago there was unmistakable evidence to more senses than one that the hospice sheltered animals as well as men. The first night my party stayed there, thunder, lightning, wind and snow gave us a boisterous welcome. Several windows were blown in and though the heads of the beds in which my sons were sleeping were at the greatest possible distance from where the window had been, the snow blew straight upon their faces. That would not happen now; a hospice that caters for those who arrive in elegant saloons and not in worn out shoes must modernise itself. A pedigree St. Bernard dog that came to help a motorist is more likely to be kidnapped than to effect a rescue.

On the south side of the pass it is hard to believe one is not yet in Italy, when the name of the valley is Poschiavo. The road and railway separate widely and it is the latter that has the best views, particularly, the view from the Grüm alp of the Palu Glacier and the fertile valley and lake of Poschiavo far below. In this farthest corner beyond her natural frontier, Switzerland possesses a small gem in Le Prese, on the shore of the lake, which seems specially placed there to provide a restful contrast to the strenuous enjoyment of the Alps, a swim in water that refreshes but does not bite, perfect peace if you row out upon its surface after dinner, and abundance of fresh trout for any meal you like.

Separated from the main Bernina group by the Val Malenco and the Muretto Pass is an outlying Alpine district greatly beloved by those who know it, but frequented mainly by Italians. It divides itself naturally into three: the Monte della Disgrazia, the highest and most important and also one of the easiest to climb; the peaks at the head of the Forno Glacier, which can be easily approached from the Maloja; and the Bondasca peaks, the most famous of which is the Piz Badile, whose immense north face of smooth rock has afforded good opportunities for proving that men with hammers and iron pitons can go where men without them cannot.

South of this part of the central chain is a long trough, whose original continuity can be traced in the Val Tellina, the Aprica Pass, the upper Valcamonica, the Tonale Pass and the Val di Sole. This trough divides the central chain from a southern chain which begins east of Como in the Bergamesque Alps and continues in the Adamello and Brenta groups and further east in the Dolomites. The Bergamesque Alps are insignificant by summer standards; in early spring they become attractive snow mountains which any visitor is likely to have almost entirely to himself. The Adamello group is high enough to carry a quite extensive glacier on its broad flat head and asserts itself sufficiently to give its own name to the group instead of the Presanella which is slightly higher. Judging by a late experience of my own, an English party in the Adamello only appears at intervals of several years. The motorcar has greatly increased the facilities for visits to outlying groups of this sort. Very careful driving and fairly dry weather are needed if you take your car to the end of the roadlet that ascends beyond the village of Saviore on the way to the Rifugio Salarno below the highest peak of the Adamello; and you may find your batteries have mysteriously run down when you come down to where you parked it.

The upper valley of the Sarca divides the granitic Adamello group obviously as well as geologically from the Brenta group. There is a road up the valley past Pinzolo to a low pass which leads into the Val Selva and so into the Val di Sole. Near the pass, beautifully placed among trees and meadows, but unfortunately out of sight of the best peaks is Madonna di Campiglio, whose hotels, the vast and the small, are filled with Italian visitors in summer.

In shape and substance the peaks of the Brenta group are dolomites. The highest, the Cima Tosa is the only one that carries a considerable amount of summer snow, and it is the easiest to climb. You have only to look at most of the others, the Crozzon, the Guglia and Fulmini di Brenta to see that they are meant for good or for rash rock climbers. If possible, any active visitor should go from Pinzolo or Campiglio to Molveno by the Bocca di Brenta. The views are grand, the surroundings on both sides are lovely, and the gateway of the pass with its colossal walls of limestone on either hand is wonderful, while the lake of Molveno is just the place in which a man should end a journey.

102 The Bernina Group from the North, showing the
Piz Bernina (*left*) and Piz Roseg

103 Eastern Peaks of the Bernina Group

104 The Crozzon di Brenta, among the most westerly Dolomites

The southern range, though it never attains a greater height than it does in the Adamello group (over 11,600 feet), is far more famous and spectacular in its continuation further east, the Dolomites of South Tyrol. The northern range, on the other hand, which has risen to such grandeur in the Bernese Oberland, diminishes steadily in importance. East of the Rhine it does not reach 10,000 feet anywhere, and only one or two peaks, the Scesaplana and the Kaltenberg carry toy glaciers.

The whole range north of the valley of the Vorder Rhein from the Oberalp Pass to Chur is often included in the Tödi group. Properly the name belongs to the fine mass of mountains at its western end of which the Tödi is the highest and is nearly 12,000 feet high. It was one of the earliest parts of the Alps to be explored, many of the snow peaks having been climbed by a monk of Disentis, Placidus a Spescha, who was an ardent disciple of Saussure, a scientist, a botanist and a mountaineer. Disentis, where passes from all directions meet, is a good centre for this district.

Two other valleys provide a beautiful approach to the recesses of the Tödi group from west and north. On the west the Maderanertal is entered from Amsteg on the St. Gotthard line. There is not yet a road up it, and it is particularly rich in vegetation and in waterfalls, in which the pessimist will see a warning of a too abundant rainfall. On the north, the railway and the road up the Lintthal bring up crowds at week-ends and in summer holidays from northern Switzerland. The defile above Thierfehd which leads to the Sandalp or the Fridolin hut, with the precipices of the Selbsanft rising 5,000 feet above, is one of the grandest in the Alps. There is a club hut in this district wherever any reasonable man could want one.

Further east Flims on the south and Elm on the north of the range are both well placed for expeditions at over 3,000 feet. Elm is the scene of a great alpine tragedy which occurred on September 11th, 1881; there are people living there who remember the horror of that Sunday afternoon, and we have detailed accounts of how it happened. The story is a striking example of the way long habit dulls the realisation of imminent danger.

Between two of the valleys that open into the hills at the south end of the basin in which Elm lies there rose a steep buttress about 1,500 feet high, with a flat top covered with trees, called the Plattenbergkopf. It was found to contain a bed of fine slate, and in 1868 a company was given a mining concession to get it out. No restrictions as to methods were laid down and a slit 600 feet broad was made which was carried 200 feet into the mountain. In 1878 the village commune took over the quarrying rights. A crack appeared in the ground behind the Plattenbergkopf, and by August 1881 it was more than four yards in width and absorbed all the water that drained down from the slopes above. A spell of very wet weather set in at the end of August, and on the 7th rocks began to fall and ominous uncomfortable sounds came from inside the mountain. Work was stopped in the quarry. On the 10th a commission from the village went up to investigate and reported that there was no immediate danger, but recommended that quarrying should cease until the spring. This aroused protests from the men who earned wages working in the quarry when bad weather made work in the fields impossible.

Next day, Sunday 11th, rocks were seen coming down frequently; the boys of the village were with difficulty held back from going up to have a closer look at what was happening. In the afternoon a group of men at the inn were watching the falls and the schoolmaster was timing their frequency, watch in hand, when suddenly a great piece of the mountain on the east side broke away and crashed down over the streams to within a few yards of where the watchers stood. No one was actually killed by this fall, but it made the villagers wonder whether, after all, they were completely safe! Those in the houses nearest the quarry began to get out some of their possessions and move the old or infirm folk. And then, seventeen minutes after the first fall, came a second, larger fall from the west side of the Plattenbergkopf. It obliterated the inn and the houses near it and killed everyone who had not left them.

This time the villagers fled in terror as hard as they could to the slopes of the Düniberg opposite, and it was there that the final fall caught them. The two falls had made vast gashes each side of the Plattenbergkopf which now joined below it, and four minutes after the second fall the whole unsupported mass came down. It must have been an unforgettable sight. The trees on the top seemed to crumple together and be swallowed in the moving summit. The whole immense mass shot down on to the slopes below, and from them bounded like a ball across the valley on to the Düniberg. Watchers lower down the valley could see clearly underneath the black flying cloud that had been a mountain a moment before. Only six persons on the Düniberg escaped, miraculously carried out of reach of the avalanche, without being killed, by the wind

105 The Bregaglia Group

106 The Bondasca Group
under fresh snow

107 The Zugspitze and Eibsee

108 The Maderanerthal

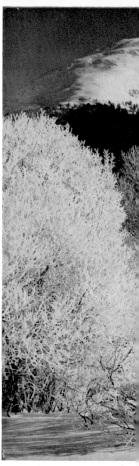

109 Winter in

110 On a 1

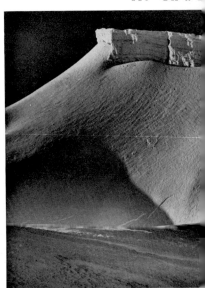

111   Piz Palu in the Bernina Group

112   The Linthal and Tödi Group

ne near Samaden

Sella Group

113 Soglio in the Val Bregaglia with the Bondasca Group

114 Pontresina and the Roseg Valley

that preceded it and blew away the roofs and then the houses themselves. It was only when the avalanche struck the Düniberg and was deflected from it down the valley that the people in the lower village realised their peril. Like a river in flood it swept over the meadows wrapped in a black cloud of dust. The village padre who was watching could hardly believe his eyes when the cloud cleared and he saw that half the lower village and 200 acres of meadow lay under a shroud of grey rocks forty feet thick.

Though there are no Alps that can be called snow mountains in the continuation of the northern range where it runs to the north of the Arlberg railway and the Inn valley, it provides some of the highest precipices in Europe and a considerable proportion of the annual death-roll from climbing accidents. The southern faces of the Dachstein and the Watzmann have been the scene of some terrific battles, even in winter, when the ice that hangs upon them might well warn off any but suicides. The Zugspitze, which was the highest peak in Germany before the annexation of Austria, and the Parseierspitze which is the highest point of all this part of the range, have been tamed by means of iron chains and blasting into mountain pets for the non-climbing tourist. Further east still, within easy reach of both Munich and Innsbruck is the Kaisergebirge, the vertical playground of the modern Munich School of climbing. This school has for some time had a large Italian class and a very much smaller English class. The chief rock walls of this range abound in "grade six" climbs, beyond the limit of what man can get up without artificial aids. The illustrations (figs. 14, 27, 28) will give some idea of this playground and the advanced climbing practised there.

Between the Bernina Pass and the Brenner, which was the eastern limit of the central range for this chapter, are two important groups of snowy Alps, the Ortler group and the Oetztal and Stubaier groups. The Stelvio Pass leading from the Val Tellina to the upper Adige valley is the natural but not the political frontier between Italy and her German speaking neighbour. The ascent on the south side is rather dull for a pass of this great height, and the view of the Ortler which bursts upon the traveller on reaching the pass is all the more impressive. The eleven miles of descent to Trafoi, with about fifty hairpin bends and a drop of more than four thousand feet, is a wonderful bit of road-making. It affords a favourite test for powerful Italian cars; I was told the ascent from Trafoi had been done in fourteen minutes. The noise they make is very

audible from the slopes of the Ortler a couple of miles away
or more. The Ortler is a very popular climb, and an easy one,
at any rate till the slopes are bare ice. The Payerhütte, from
which the easiest route starts, is on the ridge between Trafoi
and Sulden (Solda now). It is a hotel, rather than a hut. The
scraps from it must be plentiful, for I have never seen so many
Alpine choughs as I saw collected round it.

Sulden is more attractive than Trafoi, partly because the
road goes up to it and not through it, and also because the
Königsspitze, the most beautiful peak in all the Tyrolese Alps
rises close to it. You will not find it on an Italian map for it
has been re-christened Gran Zebru! The Cevedale is a grand
walk, and being detached at the far south-eastern end of the
group commands a superb view. You can sleep at a large hut at
well over 10,000 feet at the edge of a broad level uncrevassed
glacier, and it is across this that you approach the peak, thread-
ing your way through innumerable ski-ers who find here one
of the few ski-ing grounds that are pleasurable in August.

The long Oetztal running up from the Inn valley divides the
last big group of snowy Alps west of the Brenner into Oetztaler
and Stubaier Alps. In recent years, with the growth of winter
sports and favourable exchange, the two high villages Vent
and Obergurgl, each at the head of an upper branch of the
valley, had become popular resorts for English visitors.

The Oetztal contains the highest peaks, two of them, the
Wildspitz and the Weisskugel, being over 12,000 feet, and the
largest glaciers, two of them more than six miles long. The
three and a half miles of the Uebeltal Glacier, the biggest of the
Stubaier Alps, makes a poor showing beside them, but it can
boast of four climbing huts. In both groups the peaks are
rounded and stunted compared with the peaks of the Western
Alps, and are generally easy of access. They have, however,
especially those of the Stubai group, steep faces on which parties
can find a satisfying thrill of danger, if they are inclined that
way.

115　The Churfürsten Group above the Wallensee

116 Obergurgl in Winter

117 Gran Zebru (formerly Königsspitze) in the Ortler Group

VII

EASTERN ALPS

To most English people Eastern Alps mean the Dolomites. The central range does, however, continue for a distance of over 80 miles in a chain of peaks that rise well above the snow-line. First, beyond the Brenner, come the Zillertal Alps, then the chain of the Hohe Tauern. The latter name comes from the passes across the watershed called Tauern, none of them snow passes, but none—till the opening of the Gross Glockner Pass four years ago—a road pass.

The Krimmler Tauern divides the Zillertal Alps from the Gross Venediger group; the Velber Tauern divides the latter from the Glockner group, and the Heiligenbluter Tauern or Hochthor—now the road pass known as the Gross Glockner Pass—separates the Glockner groups from the last of the snowy Alps, the Ankogel group. There are more than thirty peaks over 10,000 feet and considerable areas of perpetual snow, especially in the Venediger group. Nearly all the highest peaks offer easy ways to their summits, and difficult ways for those who look for them. It was on the Gross Wiesbachhorn that Toni Schmidt, one of the conquerors of the north face of the Matterhorn, was killed in trying to climb the steep icy north-west face. The highest point in Greater Germany, the Gross Glockner, has for long been one of the most crowded, if not the most crowded summit in all the Alps. It commands a fine panoramic view and everything has been done to make it easy for any but the quite infirm to see it. You may eat a hot dinner, well cooked and join in or listen to a great chorus of snores, start after a hot breakfast and be on the summit of the Glockner in an hour and a half, the final passage from the Klein Glockner into a gap and the ascent from it being secured with a wire rope and iron stanchions. And the Glockner is by no means the only summit a visit to which has been made a matter of a two or three hours walk and which has been put on a lead of ropes or chains to curb any natural savagery of disposition.

The agent which has done the taming, which has put up the huts and runs them so well, is the D.Oe.A.V. (*Deutsche und Oestereichischer Alpenverein*, the German-Austrian Alpine Club.

17   109

It is well to remember to omit the Oe now that Austria has been obliterated, temporarily if not permanently. This club numbers some score thousands compared with the few thousands of the French and the few hundreds of the English Alpine Clubs.

The first time you enter one of these huts in the German Alps, you think it must be exceptional, so well is it equipped with all possible requirements. But it is not. Here is a sample of a meal eaten in a Tyrolese hut: "a dish of ham and eggs, fried steak and potatoes, bilberry tart, and a conical flask of white wine." An Englishman's meal, though not mine! it costs $3\frac{1}{2}$ schillings (just under 3/-). No wonder such places are well patronized! In many of them only a small minority of the company will be climbers; most will be people who have come up from the valley and are going back to it, or people going from one hut to another. For these last the benefit of not having to carry any provision for meals in huts must be great and must make them long for similar benefits, when they toil with heavier sacks up the slopes of the wilder, Western Alps.

And the paths that lead up to them, and generally those that lead from them to the passes and the peaks are lavishly blazed with red and other sorts of paint. It is almost impossible to stray with these red daggers constraining you and holding you to the way. Macbeth would never cease repeating here:

'Thou marshall'st me the way that I was going.'

One is grateful for these many aids to mountain travel, and yet there is a suggestion of ordering, of marshalling which is at variance with the glorious freedom from constraint which is one of the very things we go to find among high mountains. And with the passing of all this country under Nazi rule, these splashes of paint, and all this ordered going carry a stronger suggestion than before of a menace to freedom.

> The very stones prate of my whereabout,
> And take the present horror from the time,
> Which now suits with it.

It is better to visit the Tyrolese Alps before you know the Pennines and Mont Blanc. Beside these giants of the west, these eastern snow peaks have a slightly crushed, subservient look; you will not notice this if your mind is not possessed by the recollection of those greater, prouder Alps. The Tyrolese

118 (*opposite*)
Winter Landscape near Innsbruck

119 (*above*) The Drei Zinnen (Tre Cime di Lavoredo)

120 (*top right*) The Vajolet Towers in the Rosengarten

121 (*bottom right*) Monte Pelmo from the Fiorentini Valley

122 The Pala Group of Dolomites, with the Needle of the Cimone della Pala

123 Garmisch-Partenkirchen

snow mountains are well suited also to men who find the greater height and less approachable character of the Western Alps demand too many hours of strenuous effort. In Tyrol you can plan a succession of climbs from well-placed huts, none of which need occupy more than a few hours.

Do not expect better weather as you get further east. Conway, when he travelled right through the Alps experienced vile weather and icy winds in August in the Tyrol. That was largely the luck of the season, but there is plenty of evidence that at least in the more northerly parts of this district weather is worse than in the South-western Alps, though not worse than in the Bernese Oberland. Further south, in the Dolomites and Julian Alps the traveller will be more often warm. For one thing the peaks are lower, and severity of weather in summer depends primarily on the height at which you are.

Hitherto, one of the greatest attractions of the Tyrolese Alps has been the Tyrolese folk, kind and free and laughter-loving. It is easy to see in much that has been written in praise of Tyrolese mountains how the warmth of scenic appreciation has been increased by the delightful Austrians, female and male, encountered on the path or in the hut. The guardian of the hut, the wife who cooks, the daughter who waits are such patient, capable and often charming hosts. Let us hope they will be permitted to remain so; that the unchanging hills among which they live will keep them free from the infection of bullying intolerance which spreads so easily in cities and is broadcast through the air.

Now a few words about the Dolomites. Only a few words, for the appeal of these immense columns of rock, rising dramatically above the valleys, is essentially spectacular; a photograph is better than any attempt at description. And being so spectacular, this Dolomite country is admirably suited to the man who wishes to see the Alps from the seat of a car. Good roads run through it in many directions. It has passed more quickly and completely than any other part of the Alps from a primitive land bristling with unclimbed spires of rock to a land of roads and cars and modern hotels where every peak has been climbed, tariffed, and put in its proper class in the all-important scale of difficulty.

For all that, the first sight of this country will give to anyone who is at all scenically minded an impression not unlike that which Leslie Stephen felt when he visited Primiero seventy years ago. "The Dolomite country appears to me to be properly speaking a hill, rather than a mountain district—a region of green meadows and sparkling waters. These great masses of bare discoloured rock have somehow been intruded by diabolical art, and in short, seem to be mountains bewitched rather than mountains due to the ordinary forces of upheaval and erosion." But the development of the last seventy years has hardly been in strict accordance with the wishes he expressed: "I hoped at the time that some (of the peaks) might turn out to be inaccessible. . . . Yet when all the peaks are climbed, Primiero will be scarcely less attractive than of old. . . . I will oppose carriage roads tooth and nail; no newspapers shall be admitted within six months of their publication; if possible the post office shall be put down; all imports shall be forbidden, except, indeed, a little foreign tobacco; and the Primierians shall eat their own mutton and be clothed with their own fleeces." With regard to imports and clothes the Four-Year Plan is doing much to carry out these wishes, and democratic newspapers are, no doubt, delayed occasionally, but these are only temporary retrogressions.

Ten years after Stephen's visit, that heaviest and noblest of living mountaineers, Dr. Julius Kugy, with two of the famous Zsigmondy brothers and led by Michel Innerkofler climbed the Grosse Zinne, the highest point of the three-peaked Drei Zinnen, best known of all the Dolomites. You see it rising like a gigantic trident in the north-east from the Misurina Lake. He says: "We looked up to the precipitous Kleine (Zinne) Michel told us that it was inaccessible. Emil contradicted him, and got back the historic answer: '*Ja, wannst Flügel hatt'st!*' (Yes, when you have wings.) Less than twenty years later the Kleine Zinne has become a two hours scramble. The famous traverse on it had been described in a book on the Dolomites (advertised, no doubt inadvertently, in a leading weekly under the heading Fiction) as having "absolutely no safe hand grip from end to end" and as being 100 yards long. This view changed a short time after. "I can see no special danger here; if a climber wants to tumble off it he easily can, and in that case would commit murder as well as suicide."

The Drei Zinnen passed into Italian hands by the Treaty of Versailles and disappeared from the map; they re-appeared as the Cime di Lavaredo and the hall-mark of the new Italy was stamped upon them a few years ago when the sheer north face of the Grosse Zinne was climbed by a party of Italian guides, who used 1,300 feet of rope, 90 iron spikes and 60 clasp-rings in doing so. This is still considered quite a difficult climb, and it may perhaps call a halt in the development of Dolomite climbing, though no new generation of climbers has ever yet accepted anything the old generation has done as the last word in skill or daring. The trouble is that no peak worthy of the name in the Alps, not even a Dolomite, is bigger at the top than the bottom, and therefore when the really perpendicular precipice has been climbed, the future star performer has nothing steeper to attack.

Fortunately these towers remain what they have always been for those who are content to look and wonder at them, and watch their colours change as the glare of daylight passes into evening or distance draws over them a veil of mystery.

The slopes immediately below the perpendicular walls of these dolomite towers are generally slippery limestone scree, blinding white in the midday sun and waterless. Where there is no path they are bad to walk upon. Lower down, where the water is nearer to the surface, the flowers must find just the sort of nourishment and conditions that suit them, for the sheets of early blooms in the Tyrol have long been the delight of artists and of botanists, and of all who are neither and wonder at them. And even a botanist, seeing these myriads of blooms, almost completely hiding the green floor on which they stand, must for once forget to look for rarity in such a glory of profusion. There is proof enough here that the flowers which love lime are far greater in number than those which hate it!

On the other hand, on the sheer arid Dolomite precipices the climber will less often than elsewhere come upon the charming, lonely flowers that grow far up above the pastures on small shelves and in crevices where they seem to have been waiting for discovery, especially by him. In other parts of the Alps the rocks are generally less smooth and sheer, and melting snow above keeps up the constant supply of moisture which the roots require.

A drive along the fine road from Bolzano to Misurina will bring you close to several of the typical attractions of this country. The Karer See is close to the road on your right as you approach the Karer Pass, a clear green lake with the jagged ridge of the Latemar beyond it. There may be scores of others looking at it when you reach it, but lakes and mountains, like beautiful princesses, are not less beautiful because thousands look at them, though a private interview may be altogether more exciting.

Some of the Rosengarten peaks are on your left as you approach Vigo and the Val Fassa. Soon after, the Vajolet

18

valley opens on the left. You do not quite see the spectacular group of towers at its head, the Vajolet-thürme, on which lovers of the vertical have every chance of testing their skill and nerve and speed. If you cannot "do" the famous trio, the Winkler, Stabeler and Delago towers in a few hours, you are well outside the first class of present day cragsmen.

At the Pordoi Pass the highest point of the road is reached. It is a wonderful spot. The Rosengarten and the Langkofel are the biggest in a gathering of Dolomite peaks, while the pastures round must be very attractive to the loafer and the botanist. I had a rather less pleasant proof of the choiceness of this place when I paid for tea. The price of a cake was the highest I have ever paid, higher even than that charged at the big tea-shop in Pontresina, which suggests urban extravagance in all but its name. As the road descends to Cortina the immense wall of Tofana towers above it, a savage thing to be so near such a place; for Cortina seems to have made every effort to look as urban and modern as possible. It is not far on over the Tre Croci Pass and under the huge cliffs of Monte Cristallo to the Misurina Lake and its large hotel. Monte Sorapis faces you in one direction, the Drei Zinnen in the other; the place offers an almost too perfectly arranged display of Dolomite attractions.

Other roads traverse the district in all directions. It seems almost wrong that without the slightest effort on his part, a traveller can sit back in his car and enjoy the floral riches of San Martino di Castrozza, and sunset on the Saas Maor, the Lago d'Alleghe and the crags of Monte Civetta reflected in its green waters and a host of similar delights. But the Dolomites are like other theatrical beauties in this, that they like to give people the chance to look at them.

Where do the Eastern Alps end? Many answers might be given. For the same reason that the Ligurian Alps east of the Col di Tenda were excluded at the beginning, everything east of the Hohe Tauern and the Dolomites will be excluded now —with one exception, the Julian Alps. The tiny glaciers that exist on Triglav, the highest point, and on the Kanin shall serve as an excuse for saying a word or two about this attractive district. The fame of mountains, like the fame of men and women owes much to the minstrel who has sung their praises. And most Englishmen who have visited the Julians have gone there prepared to love them because of what Dr. Julius Kugy has written of them.

They are not fantastic as are the Dolomites. There is no

peak there, not even the precipitous Montasch, that does not look like a natural feature of the bit of country from which it has been carved. The valley floors are low, low enough to be covered with trees of every kind; and there are charming woodland rides, for example on the way up to the Manhart hut from near the Predil Pass. On the Manhart itself you may find the lovely pink *potentilla nitida*. And if you do find it, behave as Dr. Kugy urges should be done in the case of edelweiss: "Spare it! Leave to the mountains you love the noblest of their jewels! Why should it wither in yout hat? . . . It is no glory to you, it accuses you before all the mountains as a barbarous robber."

There is a road now from Tarvisio past the Raibl Lake to Nevea and Chiusaforte. Do not read what Dr. Kugy says about the beauty of Nevea when he first knew it; it may prevent your doing justice to the beauty that remains. Even from this, its easiest side, the Montasch presents such an impressive limestone face that it is difficult to believe it can be the easy climb it proves on closer acquaintance. The Kanin on the opposite side of the valley is also a fairly easy ascent, and it shares with the Maritime Alps at the other end of the Alpine chain the advantage of a seaward view. The rocky coast of Istria can be seen, the delta of the Isonzo and perhaps a glimpse of something in which fancy may help a strictly scientific vision to see Venice.

Annexation by Italy has resulted in changes in many of the names of places, peaks and passes, but the changes are generally so small that identification with the old name is easy. The barbed wire entanglements that extend across the meadows on each side of the road east of Tarvisio where it enters Jugoslavia are as ridiculously useless as they are repulsive to look at.

You may think the Eastern Alps have occupied less than their fair share of this book. In justification let me end by quoting Dr. Kugy, who was born in the Trentino and loves them. "The splendid combination of rock, ice and snow in the Western Alps provides an incomparably greater and richer field for the mountaineer than the detailed work on Dolomite towers . . . they give also a far richer reward; a landscape greater and more varied, and furthermore the fascination of the eternal snows, and of greater absolute height."

It is these last that have always counted and will always count most in a great mountain range. Travellers return from the Polar Regions and write of the varied beauty of form and colour taken by the snows and of the silent mysterious movements of huge masses of ice. In the Himalaya they may feel the extraordinary freedom from the ties and limitations of the plains conferred by great height, whether we are looking down or up. These distant parts of the earth have the advantage of emphasis and exaggeration. One has only to listen to a speech by Hitler to see how crowds may be affected by emphatic declamation. The Alps convey it all in gentler tones than Everest or the Poles, but they are not less beautiful or less full of meaning for being at our door instead of thousands of miles away. The more we know them, the better they satisfy our needs.

124 Mandlwand in the
     Allgäuer Alps

125 Hanging on in
     the Dolomites

126 At Cortina d'Ampezzo

127 Winter ending,
       Dolomites

128 The Karersee in the Latemar Group

129 The Styrian Alps

130 The Königssee near Berchtesgaden

131 Triglav

INDEX

The numerals in heavy type refer to the figure numbers of illustrations.

Abriès, 42
Adamello Group, 104
Adelboden, 73
Aiguilles, 26; **56**
Aiguilles d'Arves, 47
Aiguille de Bionassay, 56, 67; **65**
Aiguille de Blaitière, 56; **50, 59**
Aiguille de la Za, 93; **95**
Aiguille du Midi, 56, 61; **58**
Aiguille du Plan, 56
Aiguille Noire de Peuteret, 66
Aiguilles Rouges, 23, 57, 58, 71
Aletschhorn, 22, 81
Allgäuer Alps, **30, 124**
Almer, Ulrich, 90
Alps, character of, 1–4
    history, 29, 30
    races of, 29
Altels, **72**
Animals, 19, 20; **18-21**
Arenaria Grandiflora, **15**
Argentera, 36, 38
Arolla, 11, 91, 94; **92**

Balmat, Jacques, 30
Balmhorn, 76; **72**
Belalp, 13, 82
Bell, Miss Gertrude, 80
Belledonne Range, 47
Belloc, Mr., 99
Bergamesque Alps, 104
Bergschrund, 11; **8**
Bernese Alps, 72–84; **68, 73**
Bernese Oberland, 5, 6, 7, 77–84
Bernina, 5, 22; **98**
Bernina Group, 101–3; **102, 103**
Besimauda, 37
Bessano, **34**
Dettmer Alp, **81**
Beuil, 39, 40
Bietschhorn, 23, 81, 82; **76**
Bionnassay, 62
Birds, 21; **22**
Bisse (watercourse) 76; **64**
Blaitière, **50, 59**
Blausee (Lukmanier Pass), **99**
Blumlisalp, 78, 81; **66**
Bobbio, 44
Bondasca Peaks, 103; **29, 106, 113**

Bonneval, 47, 48, 52
Bordeaux, M. Henri, 52
Bouquetins, 19; **19**
Brèche de la Meige, **39**
Bregaglia Group, **105**
Brenner Pass, 6
Brenta Group, 104
Brenva, 53, 67, 68
Brévent, 17, 58
Brown, Dr. Graham, 68
Burgener, Alexander, 55

Casteldelfino, 41, 44
Central Alps, 25, 97–108
Cérésole, 52
Certosa di Pesio, 37
Cevedale, 108
Chamois, 19, 21; **18**
Chamois hunter, **17**
Chanrion, 92
Charmoz, 55, 58, 65; **50, 53**
Château d'Oex, 73
Chécroui Alp, 67; **60**
Cheese-making, **32**
Churfürsten Group, **115**
Cima dei Geilas, 38
Cima Tosa, 104
Cimone della Pala, **122**
Ciseaux, **57**
Climbing, 24–9, 78, 85, 87, 107; **14
    27, 77, 125**
    Equipment, 25, 28; **27**
Cogne, 11, 19, 31, 47, 48, 49; **44**
Col de Larche, 40, 41
Col de la Seigne, 64
Col du Géant, 61, 71
Concordia, 79–81; **7**
Contamines, 61, 62
Conway, Sir Martin, 32
Coolidge, Professor, 44
Cornstooks, Tyrolean, **26**
Cortina, 2, 114; **126**
Cottian Alps, 41–5
Courmayeur, 24, 53, 61, 66
Cresta Avers, 31; **31**
Cresta Maloja, **100**
Crétins, 74
Crissola, 43
Crocus, **16**
Crozzon di Brenta, **104**

Dachstein, 107
Dauphiné Alps, 6, 7, 45–7
Dent Blanche, 23, 90, 91; **88**
Dents du Midi, 71
Denudation *v.* Erosion
Deutsche und Oestereichischer Alpen-verein, 109
Diablerets, 73, 75
Dolomites, 5, 13, 23, 101, 111–14; **23, 123, 127**
Dom, **87, 94**
Dôme, 60
Douves Blanches, 11
Dragons, 20
Drei Zinnen, 30, 112, 114; **119**
Dru, **51**
Düniberg, 106, 107

Eagles, 20; **22**
Eastern Alps, 5, 17, 24, 26, 109–16
Ecrins, 36, 46; **38**
Egginerjoch, **94**
Eibsee, **107**
Eiger, 1, 5, 24, 77, 78; **77, 78, 80**
Eigerwand, 78
Elm, 105
Engadine, **109**
Erosion, 5 ff.
Everest, 1, 116

Fafleralp, 81, 82
Fauteuil des Allemands, 67; **60**
Fiéry, 95
Fiorentini Valley, 121
Fionnay, 92
Finsteraarhorn, 26, 80
Flégère, 58
Fletschhorn, **81, 89**
Flims, 105
Flowers, Alpine, 15–18, 37, 39, 115; **15, 16**
Fluhalp, 88, 89
Föhn, 77
Fou, **51**

Gabelhorn, 91
Garmisch-Partenkirchen, **123**
Gasterental, 81
Geneva, Lake of, 8
Geology of the Alps, viii, 4–9, 98
Georges, Joseph and Antoine, Guides, 90
Glaciers, 3, 7, 10, 12–14; **3, 11**
    Aletsch, 13, 23, 32, 81; **67, 69**
    Blanc, 46
    Bossons, 12
    Brenva, 14, 65
    Ciardoney, 11
    des Agneaux, **42**
    des Glaciers, 64

Fischer, **83**
Géant, 11
Grenz, 11
Grimsel, 17
Mer de Glace, 55, 58, 61; **49, 53**
Miage, 12, 65, 67
Morteratsch, 101, 103; **25**
Oberaar, 80
Oberaletsch, 82
Pasterze, 13; **13**
Gletsch, **82**
Goitre, 74
Gordalasca, 38, 39
Gornergrat, 88
Gos, Charles, 35
Graian Alps, 18, 47–52
Grandes Jorasses, 24, 58; **6, 49, 53, 61**
Gran Paradiso, 18, 36, 49, 50
Gran Zebru, *v.* Königsspitze
Grauson Valley, 51
Grépon, 55, 65; **54**
Gressonez, 95
Grimsel, 17, 80; **82**
Grindelwald, 32, 77, 78
Grivel, Henri, 67
Grivola, 23, 48; **43**
Gross Glockner, 5, 13, 109; **13**
Gross Venediger, 5
Grunsee, 83
Gstad, 73
Gsteig, 73
Guides, 27
Guil Valley, 41, 42

Haslital, 83
Haymaking, **30, 31**
Herbetet, 49, 50
Himalaya, 1
Hohe Tauern, 5, 109, 114
Horn, Alpine, **25**
Hudson, Charles, 60
Hunting, 19, 50

Inscriptions on chalets, 33, 34

Javelle, Emile, 71
Jones, Owen Glynne, 91
Julian Alps, 5, 114, 115
Juf, 31; **31**
Jungfrau, 26, 78, 80; **70, 78, 80**
Jungfraujoch, 13, 79; **7, 8**
Jura, the, 8

Kaisergebirge, 25, 101; **27**
Kaiserthal, **4, 5**
Kandersteg, 83
Kanin, 114, 115
Karabiner, 25; **27**
Karer See, 113; **128**
Kienthal, **71**

Kippel, 82
Klücker, 102
Königssee, **130**
Königsspitze, 108; **117**
Kugy, Dr. Julius, 53, 112, 114, 115

Lac Blanc, **56**
Lac Bleu, 93
La Fouly, 69
La Grave, 46; **36**
Lammergeier, 20
Langkofel, 114; **23**
La Lex Blanche, 63, 66
Laquinhorn, 89; **89**
Larden, Mr. Walter, 33
Latemar, 113; **128**
Lauterbrunnen, 79; **74**
Le Lautaret, 17, 18, 46
Le Prese, 103
Lenk, 73
Lepontine Alps, 97–101
La Flégère, **52**
Les Houches, 61, 62
Les Mottets, 63, 64
Levanna, 36
Ligurian Alps, 114
Lillaz, **48**
Linthal, **112**
Lo Besso, **90**
Lochmatter, Franz, 87
Lötschental, 20, 23, 33, 72, 77, 80, 81, 82; **75**
Lucerne, 20
Lyskamm, 11, 87, 88; **91**

Maderanertal, 105; **108**
Maljasset, 42
Mallory, 1
Maloja, 7
Mandlwand, **124**
Maritime Alps, 15
Märjelensee, 83; **67**
Marmolata, 13
Marmots, 19; **21**
Martigny, 6, 8, 54
Mason, Mr. A. E. W., 68
Matterhorn, 9, 26, 85, 96; **2, 84, 86**
Mauerhaken, 25; **27**
Meije, 26, 45; **36**
Meiringen, 77
Meyer family, 26
Mischabel Peaks, 23, 89; **81**
Mönch, **78, 80**
Montana, 76
Montasch, 115
Mont Blanc, 4, 7, 13, 14, 23, 53, 54; **1, 52, 56, 59, 60, 62, 63**
Mont Blanc Range, 53–71
Mont Clapier, 37, 38, 39
Mont Collon, 93; **92**

Monte Cristallo, 114
Monte della Disgrazia, 103
Montenvers, 55; **49**
Monte Leone, 99
Monte Pelmo, **121**
Monte Rosa, 5, 8, 9, 85, 87; **85**
Monte Viso, 36, 41; **42**
Mont Maudit, 4, 11
Mont Pelat, 40
Mont Pelvoux, **41**
Motoring, 2, 39, 42, 48, 90
Mummery, A. J., 55, 56
Mummery Crack, 55; **54**
Munich School of Climbers, 25, 107
Murren, 24

Nadelhorn, **87**
Névé, 10

Ober Aarhorn, **83**
Obergabelhorn, **90**
Obergurgl, 108; **116**
Oeschinsee, 83; **66**
Oetztal Group, 107, 108
Ormsby, John, 72
Ortler Group, 107, 108

Pala Group, **122**
Passes
    Albula, 101
    Beich, 82
    Ferden, 77
    Forclaz, 54
    Furka, 6
    Gemmi, 73, 76
    Gries, 97, 98
    Grimsel, 17, 80; **82**
    Gross Glockner, 109
    Lötschen, 73
    Lukmanier, 99, 100; **99**
    Mont Cenis, 41
    Moro, 30
    Pordoi, 17
    St. Bernard, 30
    St. Gotthard, 83
    Sella, 102
    Simplon, 97, 99
    Splügen, 99
    Stelvio, 107
Peasant Life, 31 ff.
Pelvo d'Elva, 44
Pelvoux, Mont, 46; **41**
Pennine Alps, 85–96
Petit Clocher de Planereuse, 70; **55**
Piz d'Aela, 101
Piz Palu, 102, 103; **9, 111**
Pizzo Bianco, 102; **98**
Plan, **50**
Planpraz, 57, 58
Plattenbergkopf, 105

Po, 7, 41, 43
Pointe Percée, **62**
Political Frontiers, 29 ff., 34, 61
Pontresina, 19; **114**
Pralognan, **46**
Praz de Fort, 70
Ptarmigan, 21
Punta de Cian, 94
Pyramides Calcaires, 64

Red-winged wall-creeper, 21
Rey, Guido, 43, 95
    house of, **86**
Rhone, 6, 7, 8, 23
Richards, I. A., 90
Ried, 81, 82
Riederalp, 13, 23, 82
Riffelalp, 24
Riffelsee, 88; **84**
Rifugio Torino, 67
Rigi, 6; **12**
Rimpfischhorn, 88
Roccia del Abisso, 15, 38
Roccia Viva, **47**
Roseg Valley, 19, 22, 101, 102; **96, 114**
Rosengarten Peaks, 113
Rothhorn, 87, 91
Ruitor, 52

Saas Fee, 8, 24, 89; **89**
Saas Valley, 8, 13
St. Martin de Vésubie, 39; **35**
St. Moritz, 2
St. Sauveur, 39, 40
Saleinaz Hut, 70
Samaden, 6; **109**
San Dalmazzo di Tenda, 15
Saussure, 4, 26, 53, 57, 60
Scheidegg, Grosse, 77; Kleine, **79**
Schmidt, Franz and Toni, 87, 109
Schwarzsee, 83
Sella Group, **110**
Séracs, **10**
Sestrières, 45
Shelley, 4, 53
Ski-ing, 14
Smythe, Mr. Frank, 68
Snow, 8 ff., 14, 37
Snow-finch, 21
Soglio, **29, 113**
South-Western Alps, 36–52
Splugen, 31
Stephen, Leslie, 111
Structure of the Alps, viii, 4–9 and
    v. also Geology.
Stubaier Alps, 107, 108
Styrian Alps, **129**
Symonds, John Addington, 32

Täschhorn, 87; **87, 94**

Téléfériques, 2, 15, 57, 62
Thun, Lake of, 83; **80**
Tödi Group, 105; **112**
Töpffer, 35
Tre Cima di Lavaredo, *v.* Drei Zinnen
Triglav, 114; **131**
Tschingelhorn, 81
Tuckett Refuge, **41**
Tyndall, Professor, 82
Tyrolese Alps, 110, 111; **26**

Ubaye Valley, 41, 42

Vajolet Towers, 113, 114; **120**
Valais Alps, **6**
Val Anzasca, 96
Val d'Anniviers, 23, 90; **90**
Val d'Aosta, 66, 67
Val de Bagnes, 91, 92
Val d'Hérens, 23, 89, 91
Val d'Isère, 47, 48; **46**
Val Ferret, 59; **61**
Val Pellice, 44, 45
Val Tanara, 37
Valleille, **48**
Vallot, Charles, 62
Vallot hut, 60
Valnontez, 49; **44**
Valpelline, 94, 95
Veglia Alp, 98
Venetz, 55
Via Mala, 100; **97**
Villar, 73
Viso, Monte, 36, 43; **42**
Visp, 8

Waldensians, 44
Wallensee, **115**
Weisshorn, 13, 23, 82, 84, 86, 90
Weisskugel, 108
Weissmies, 89
Western Alps, 24, 25, 26
Wetterhorn, 26, 77; **73, 79**
Whymper, 72, 88
Wiesener Alp, **16**
Wilder Kaiser, **27**
Wildhorn, 13, 76
Wildspitz, 108
Wildstrubel, 32, 73, 76
Wyttenwasserstock, 98

Young, Mr. Geoffrey, 24, 46, 87

Zermatt, 2, 9, 86
Zillis, 100; **101**
Zinal, 87, 91
Zinal Rothhorn, 90; **93**
Zsigmondy, the brothers, 45, 112
Zugspitze, 107; **107**
Zweisimmen, 73

Munich
Inn
L. Constance
BAVARIAN ALPS
VORARLBERG
Arlberg P.
Landeck
Innsbruck
STUBAY ALPS
TUXER ALPS
Brenner P.
Chur
RHAETIAN ALPS
ENGADINE
OETZTAL ALPS
Meran
Eisack
Stelvio P.
Pontresina
Bernina P.
ORTLER ALPS
Maloja
Bolzano
Marmolata
DOLOMITES
Avisio
Adda
Adamello
Cima Tosa
Trento
TRENTINO
L. Como
BERGAMESQUE ALPS
L. Iseo
L. Garda
VENETIAN
Milan
Verona
Venice
Adige
Po